Making Memorable Marriages

A Guide to Creating Your Unique Wedding

BY
REV. MARY MONTANARI

Copyright © Reverend Mary Montanari, 2020

Reverend Mary Montanari has asserted her right to be identified as the author of this work.

All rights reserved.

No part of this publication may be reproduced, stored in any retrieval system, or transmitted in any form, or by any means, electronic, mechanical, photocopying, recording, or otherwise, without the prior written permission of the author.

Print Book ISBN: 979-8-550636-3-29

Book Interior and E-book Design by Amit Dey | amitdey2528@gmail.com
Cover design © milagraphicartist.com

DEDICATION

To all the couples, past present and future, that I have the honour to unite in marriage.

I am so grateful for my loving parents, Felice and Mario Montanari for being brave enough to have me.

I am so grateful for my four beautiful children, Peter Michael, Matthew, Thomas and Sarah, for your support, hugs, laughs and words of encouragement.

To my dearest friend Kirsten for having faith in me and keeping me on track to getting this book completed, even during a Pandemic!

Rev. Roland and Giulio for photographic skills and Nancy Aronie for giving me the courage to put my words on paper

To all my spirit guides, angels, deceased loved ones and God/Universe for having more trust in me that I could have ever image.

TABLE OF CONTENTS

Prayer vii

Introduction ix

Chapter 1: The Many Faces of Love, My Story 1

Chapter 2: You're Engaged! Now What? 17

Chapter 3: Frequently asked questions 25

Chapter 4: Choosing Your Vows. 31

Chapter 5: Reading poetry together 43

Chapter 6: My Most Popular Traditional and Family Ceremonies . . . 53

Chapter 7: Rehearsals (or not). 86

Chapter 8: The Big Day. 92

Conclusion 103

Appendix I 105

Appendix II Services & Fees 107

Resources 111

Checklists for wedding preparation. 113

About the Author. 117

Notes 118

PRAYER

Love is more than just a word, action, feeling or object.
It comes when you surrender the ego to allow yourself to be.
Be the person you always have been and develop even more.
Love celebrates these moments with pure joy and peace.
With love, one has the patience to see beyond the chaos in front of them.
Each person in your life is your mirror.
We are here to experience life through emotions.
The more we love ourselves the more we are able to love another.
The more we understand our boundaries, the more we are able to witness life unfold in front of us.
We are a soul living a human experience through emotions.

We benefit in our relationship with others by arriving, being with that person in the moment. Listening from the heart and not by past memories of relationships and what was done then.
A key step in communications is to make no assumptions but ask the questions. Ask for clarity.

In any relationship there may come a time of growth via conflicts. If you are feeling hurt and uncertain about how to resolve the situation, step back, take time out, meditate and ask the Universe for guidance. I like to surrender my issues to God, and trust that I will be guided. This way, my emotions do not take over. The answers to your problems will arrive. I respond to a situation rather than react. The reacting ones got me into deeper trouble.

Whether you are a believer or not, we are never alone. Our guardian angel is by our sides and loves to help us. Keep the communications open. There are some wow moments in your lives where you may have wondered, 'how could this have happened because it was so amazing!' Like meeting your incredible partner!! Synchronicity and some say chance, I say your angels are helping.

Remember to make gratitude a daily practice and more good things will appear.
One couple's therapist advises their couples to say words of gratitude before going to bed. Helps to end the day with appreciation for each other.
Like attracts Like.

Enjoy the magic of the moment and accept grace when it arrives. Keep dreaming. You are worth it!

Be humble.
Be happy.

Feel your heart beating.
Feel your breath entering and exiting your body.

This is you.

Many blessings on your new journey ahead of you as a married couple.

Big hugs,

Rev Mary

INTRODUCTION

*Y*ou are now entering a very crazy time of your life marriage! Congratulations!

It takes a lot of courage to make this next move in your lives! So, I am here to help...at least with the wedding ceremony.

I have a calling to create and perform weddings. How many people can say they love their job? I do! And to boot, I was born on February the 14th, yes! A Valentine's Day baby and living the role to unite couples in love!

This book contains some helpful tools to help design your unique wedding ceremony, including some checklists at the back of the book. Over the years, I have collected poems, readings, vows, and traditional marriage ceremonies from living in the multi-cultural city of Toronto. Personal travel has also given me understanding many cultures and customs.

I hope that the following pages will delight your hearts and keep them open to share with family and loved ones the way you want to announce to the world the new Mr. and Mrs., or the new Mrs. and Mrs. or the new Mr. and Mr. or the New-Married couple. Your wedding, your way with love.

Chapter One

THE MANY FACES OF LOVE, MY STORY

Hello, I am Reverend Mary Montanari.

Before you consider hiring anyone for your wedding day, it is important to meet them. More people used to belong to a religious community and knew their leaders. They paid their weekly donations, regularly visited their place of worship and even invited their priest/ imam/rabbi/bhikkhu/ over for a family meal. All forms of religious ceremonies took place in these temples.

Today, living in a very multi-cultural city, a wedding officiant can help smooth the challenges of a multi-faith wedding or for those who no longer observe their religious traditional ceremonies or don't have a place to worship.

How does one become acquainted with a wedding officiant? Maybe through videos, conversations, social media posts, past client reviews, and personal referrals from friends who may have used their services. These are all brilliant ways to meet someone who will be part of your very special moment.

In this chapter, I want to be more personal and share with you why I love my work. It gets a little woo-woo in spots, but

I promise you, it's been an exciting and eventful journey! It has also given me a deep understanding and compassion for the many challenges in relationships, with ourselves, with others, and with a higher power. All of this has affected how I approach the sanctity of a wedding ceremony.

So here goes!

I was born to Italian Catholic immigrants, and the Church was very much in my life. It was so influential I wanted to be a priest. My mom told me that women do not become priests, but nuns. That annoyed me, as I would have conversations with the Virgin Mary and Mother Earth all the time. I thought God was too busy for me, so I preferred to communicate with His mother. As time passed on, my faith for the Church lessened with their strong negative stand on issues of same-sex marriages and abortions. It wasn't the Church that helped me out of my deepest darkest moments in my life but direct conversations with God himself.

Some people see, some people hear, some people feel, and some people just know. Well, I have a complete set of these intuitive gifts. Around the age of eight, noises coming from the kitchen in the basement, just under my bedroom, regularly woke me at 3 a.m.. The ghost that lived in my parent's home just loved cooking at that hour. It soon became too much for my little self to take. No one else could hear him, just me. Overwhelmed and scared, I asked God to stop the noise. "I don't want to listen to this anymore!" And the noise stopped, but there was a cost, I felt more of everyone's emotions around me. I can explain and understand this now but not as a child.

I mentioned in the beginning that I am a Valentine Day baby and I love Love. I have always loved to kiss. Don't misunderstand, I am not easy. First base is all I am about. As a child of ten, I would imagine what a kiss would be like when I got older. When

I became a teenager, and the hormones kicked in, kissing was on my mind and on my lips.

How I enjoyed kissing! Every fresh love interest meant a new exploration of that kiss. Some were brief kisses, let's call them the becks. Some were so wet that I needed a towel after to dry my face. Let's call them the bathers. Some were full of adventures. I had no idea where their tongues were planning to end up. Let's call them the explorers.

As I grew older, I found even more types, like the fish lips where their lips were slim. I didn't know if they could even enjoy mine. Oh, and then there were the thick lips, those were the ones I felt like I was their favorite ice cream and they couldn't stop kissing me.

Then, there was the one that made me melt. I married him in 1988 and raised four kids with those lips. Over the seventeen years of marriage, with the stress of family life and a very successful workaholic partner, the kisses became fewer and fewer. I was not wise enough then to realize the power of true self love comes from within and not from another. Assumptions, lack of self-esteem, cultural beliefs, lack of support and sleep makes one blind to reality.

Fast forward...

The year 2005 contained many ups, downs, closures and new beginnings. On my first lady's trip, in May 2005, one of the ladies shared with us her personal experience with a treatment modality called Reiki. Reiki is a massage therapy. Although there is no touching involved, one senses things happen in the body. The thought of it intrigued me. Fascinating thing about life, when you ask a question, the answer seems to arrive in divine timing. In my case, I won a weekend getaway the following month and arranged the time for the end of June when school finished with the kids..

I packed up the kids, as their dad was too busy to attend, and we drove up to a family resort in Orillia, called Ferns Inn. The kids and I had a blast. On one rainy afternoon, as the kids were in their day camps, I walked over to their spa and to my delight discovered that Reiki sessions were being offered. I booked my first Reiki session. Not only did this session wake me up to a world I was avoiding but allowed me the space to realize I had closed off. From that moment on, I kept looking to experience more healing sessions via Reiki.

In July 2005, my husband and I travelled to Majorca, Spain, for a romantic getaway. When we arrived, my back spasmed. Fortunately, their spa had an acupuncturist who helped to relieve the pain, and another Reiki practitioner. After two Reiki sessions, I realized that I too had the ability to perform this healing modality and returned to Toronto for further study.

One warm summer afternoon at the end of July 2005, when all the kids were downstairs watching television, my husband of seventeen years told me that those kisses were now for another and not mine anymore. No more kisses for Mary. My heart and lips were dry and cracked. When he left me and our four children under the age of fourteen, I was so devastated that I could not think straight for months. No one knew that my heart had been shattered, and mind filled with shame and embarrassment. My kids were my world, and I chose not to fight or limit their father's access to them. I strongly feel that the Reiki sessions helped me prepare for this new stage of my life. We created our children in love, and he will always be their dad. (He became an even better dad after the divorce.)

An interesting thing happened on a dazzling fall afternoon during my walk with my thirteen-year-old golden retriever. I was having a very serious discussion with God and basically telling him that I had had it. I will no longer be the controller of my life and I yelled at Him, "Here you have me! What the fuck am I now supposed to do?" Well that wasn't a good idea yelling at Him but at least I got his attention! I heard God's voice as if He was right within me, loud and clear. Filled with love. "Talk". I said, "What? You want me to talk?" and then He said it again, "Talk". He doesn't talk much, just that one word, and I knew it was Him. I fell into tears and felt as if a door had opened up into the strongest sunshine ever, where I was blinded by the light and cried with joy because He was listening to me all the time.

I have never looked back. From that moment on, I surrendered my life to God. I became truly His servant. Thus began my journey to self-love and forgiveness. I went back to school at the age of forty-four and took Spiritual Director and psychotherapy programs, and met and became close to a married man with a wife with MS. For the first time, I started to practice self-care. Later that year, I became a Reiki Master, undertook therapy, and traveled the world to experience life.

In January 2006, I received a sign to travel to Thailand. It was my first solo long distant trip. Here I visited several temples, argued and laughed with monks, witnessed dying rituals and learned to cook Thai food. By September 2007, I saw my lover's true colors when I witnessed how he treated his disabled wife. I could only image how he would ever treat me if the situation was reversed. Alone again, I attended my first Doreen Virtue course with her then husband, Steve Farmer, in Laguna Beach as I explored my spiritual connections further. A Dead Sea Scrolls exhibition was an hour away in San Diego CA, and I walked through that show as if a dream, deeply touched because I had been longing to see them for over a year.

In February 2008, my traveling adventures led me to Egypt and my lips to be touched by a young, tall, dark, handsome man. A new human love, and a Third deep spiritual realization. It was here in the land surrounded by deserts, heat, sweat, oasis and a unique culture that I embraced the strength of my intuition fully as I slept two miles away from the powerful pyramids. My third eye opened, and I began to understand even more about myself. Long-distance relationships are a challenge and coming from two distinct cultures is even more challenging. I would not move to Egypt, and he would not move to Canada. After a year of me traveling back and forth, this was not going any further, so we said our goodbyes.

In March 2010, while visiting Nepal and India, I had my Fourth spiritual awakening to Death. Flying over to India, a vision of Mother Teresa came to me as I was telling her I was sorry that my travel plans did not include visiting her special place in

Calcutta. Boy, are her hands big! She just smiled at me and nodded her head. Once again, I surrendered my desire. First we landed in Nepal and the day before my tour was to start, I hired a street boy to show me around and tell me that Mother Teresa had an orphanage here in Kathmandu, Nepal. The next day, my professional tour guide found the compound, filled with babies and children. A young nun invited me to pray in Mother Teresa's chapel. There on the wall were my heroes, Mother Teresa, John Paul II and Jesus! I knew I wasn't alone, kneeled and cried with happiness. She also took me to another location where older family members had been dropped off as no one wanted to take care of them. Here in North America we call then "Retirement Homes". The spaces were small and well taken care of by the many international volunteers and donations.

I have been comfortable with death and it was only natural that when witnessing families bathe and prepare their deceased

loved one's bodies by the rivers in Kathmandu, Nepal and in India I saw the burnings of the bodies in the Ganges River at Varanasi. I only saw love, compassion and tradition shine.

The biggest gift I received on that trip was hearing God speak again. Once again just a single word and I melted as I left the temple at The Isipathana Deer Park in Sarnath, India, the same place where Buddha came out of the forest after his awakening. When I exited the temple, a few locals approached me with flowers. I then led them to Buddha's offering spot to place the flowers together.

Returning from India, I felt more grounded and wanted a family life as my kids' father had remarried and started another family. I began a love relationship with a sympathetic friend in the summer of 2010. We promised that our new relationship wouldn't affect our existing friendship. We enjoyed time with both sets of kids, cooking, skiing and the challenge of keeping them active. By

mid-January of 2012, once again truth was revealed, and I ended the relationship and lost a friend.

I had already planned the trip with my last lover for March 2012 and was blessed to have his portion refunded with no effort. Thank You angels! My solo adventures took me to Jordan and Israel, where I walked in the windy Wadi Rum desert, floated in the Dead Sea, baptized my feet in the waters where the first baptism took place, and stood near the Qumran Caves where the Dead Sea scrolls were found. I saw that more will come. And to top it all, I witnessed snow fall in Jerusalem on the Holy site two days after I placed my very small piece of paper with my prayer in a crack of the Wailing Wall.

In the August of 2012, after six months of further healing of my heart, I entered a new romance. This included several trips that proved to be spiritually transformational. We had an off and on relationship that lasted several years because he kissed me like

I was his favorite ice cream, which I so needed at the time as my ex-husband had his third child with his wife.

In November 2013, we visited Turkey and our tour guide led us high in the mountains to Mother Mary's House in Izmir. I am in awe of the energy on this mountain. It was so peaceful, and the sense of calmness was so strong. As I stood there amongst some other tourists, the head priest of this chapel approached me and handed me his card. "Please come to mass tonight," he said and walked away. I thought, 'Did I just get a personal invite? I did!' We arranged with our driver, who had never heard of this happening before, to drop us off later that evening to attend the most incredible mass ever. There were only five people in Mother Mary's House. The love, the warmth, the candles burning, and so much more made the mass magical and surreal.

Once again God, who I like to call Dad or Universe, stepped into my life and led me to my wonderful Hospice volunteer job (2014) and then the ministry, Canadian International Metaphysical Ministry. On May 26th, 2015, I was ordained as a minister and then registered with the Ontario Government. This great privilege has allowed me to perform inter-faith weddings of many cultures, and same-sex marriages! Which is so cool, fun and amazing! (In the spring of 2017, I received an email from Tade Credgeur, another Toronto wedding officiant, regarding joining a team of wedding officiants for support and assistance. Her energy was so loving and fun that we instantly became friends and between us help as many couples as we can.)

In December 2016, my then partner was invited to Japan for business and I came for the ride with no expectations. Much to my surprise when we were in Kyoto, I discovered how close I was to the mountain to where Dr. Usui, who brought Reiki into the modern world, received his gifts of the Reiki modalities. I journeyed to Suginami-Ku-Umezato, to pay my respects at his tomb. I also enjoyed experiencing several tea ceremonies. I am honoured to be a Reiki Master in this life.

In May 2017, China's history with ancient teachings led me to my next adventure. We visited the Mutianyu Great Wall, Shandong (where Taoism started), the Temple of Confucius and Shaolin Temple. Next, we returned to Japan to visit and I blessed the Chou Park and Shukkeien where the atom bomb landed. The discovery that I could still taste metal in the air and that more children were killed by the atomic bomb than the world knows grieved me. I stopped and opened my heart to all those innocent souls that died and had never been acknowledged in the Western world.

In September 2017, we traveled from Ho Chi Minh City in the south of Vietnam all the way to the north where we arrived at Hanoi to experience the Vietnam culture and how the Vietnam war affects their lives more than the West knows. We discovered several of Anthony Bourdain's street food places, which were incredible! I fell in love with the rich tasting flavour of Vietnamese ice coffee and have been blessed to have several Vietnamese couples even give coffee to me as gifts later after I shared my travels .The strength of the people, their food, bike riding in the rice fields, their coffee and custom tailors helped make this country one I want to return to as soon as possible!

In April 2018, I returned with friends to Bangkok, Thailand for classes in Thai massage. Coping with jet lag and learning a new skill was challenging, but I did it!

I journeyed to Manila and Boracay in the Philippines in November 2018 to pick wedding supplies and witness a local wedding. It turned out to have more of an American flare than Philippine. This was my last trip with my love.

Unbeknownst to me, he still loved his ex-wife, and his own divorce hurt him more than he ever let on. Our frequent travels, though wonderful, came with a price. I was trying too hard to

make something work when healing still was required and being avoided by us both. I am a firm believer that if you don't address your emotions that they will manifest in your body as an illness.

I became very ill with a disease called Cold Agglutinin. The auto immune system mistakenly targets red blood cells when I am exposed to cold temperatures or stress. During this time of awareness, I revalued my life again through the power of meditation. Then I chose my life. I took better care of my body, mind and soul and focused less on fixing something I had no knowledge on how to repair. The awareness provided my nourishment, and I became stronger. This newfound self-love gave me the courage to end that relationship and start living the life I now wanted more than anything.

Which brings me to finding my true calling as a marriage officiant.

I believe in Love. I believe we are all connected and only through self-love can we love another. I believe when you are ready for love, love finds you and in the funniest of places.

I take great joy and pride to be part of uniting love. As soon as I started performing wedding ceremonies, I was living my dream! Living my life celebrating love with all. Weddings are the best place to do this!

Each couple is unique, and we create the ceremony together. My gift to each couple is that I arrive to be of service, and I am fully present. We create the sacred space for the ceremony to take place with the intention of love and peace. That is why I ask how many guests will be attending so that I may prepare. By law every wedding has certain aspects that need addressing, but that is my job. It is during a rehearsal or walk through that we sense and see how that day will unfold. We will discuss this further in Chapter 7.

Every wedding has memorable moments. The very first wedding I performed was the day my best friend Debbie died of a heart attack at fifty-five years old. I had spent the day with all my friends as we were in shock and trying to comfort each other. Very few of us knew she had heart issues. Debbie lived for everyone else. I had to take a deep breath and move through my responsibility to perform a wedding filled with joy and love no matter what. The ceremony was at 5 pm. Debbie died around 10 am. I left the party with the bride and groom dancing the night away at 9 pm with a veil over my face as no one knew what had happened a few hours before.

I performed one of my same-sex marriages in October 2018 to join two beautiful women. This was a second marriage for both of them. We had so much fun with the grandkids and family

members at the rehearsal and on the day of the wedding. I had my tissues in my hands as we were all crying with joy with their union.

By the way, I'm still friends with my ex-husband. The rest of this story, the road to self-compassion is in my next book.

Chapter Two
YOU'RE ENGAGED! NOW WHAT?

With divine guidance you met your love. You followed your heart and let synchronicity lead the way. You have made the promise and now you are making your dream real. To keep a healthy relationship growing, I have included some of my favorite books in the appendix for further reading. No matter what will happen in your journey together the best advice is to have some guidance around you. Surrounding yourselves with positive affirmations help to keep your relationship grounded and open for growth. Here are three of my favorites that I hang in my main floor bathroom to remind me daily as well as my guests. All are from H.H. The XIV Dalai Lama.

Pride
If you assume
A humble attitude,
Your own good qualities
Will increase,
Whereas when you are
Full of pride
There is no way to be happy.

You will become
Jealous of others,
Angry with them,
And look down on them,
Due to which an unpleasant
Atmosphere will be created
And unhappiness in society
Will increase.

Compassion
Usually, our concept
Of compassion or love refers
To the feeling of closeness
We have with our friends and
Loved ones. Sometimes
Compassion also carries a
Sense of pity. This is wrong
Any love or compassion which
Entails looking down on the other
Is not genuine compassion.
To be genuine compassion must
Be based on respect for the other,
And on the realization that others
Have the right to be happy and
Overcome suffering, just
As much as you. On this basis,
Since you can see that others are
Suffering, you develop a genuine
Sense of concern for them.

Selfishness
We can also approach
The importance of compassion
Through intelligent reasoning.
If I help another person,
And show concerns for
Him or her, then I myself
Will benefit from that.
However, if I harm others,
Eventually I will be in trouble.
I often joke, half sincerely
And half seriously, saying
That if we wish to be truly selfish,
Then we should be wisely selfish
Rather than foolishly selfish.
Our intelligence can help
To adjust our attitude in this
Respect. If we use it well,
We can gain insights as to
How we can fulfill our own
Self-interest by leading a
Compassionate way of life.

And then of course there is always, the Bible, Matthew 6.14-7

Judging Others
Do not judge, so that you may not be judged. For with the judgement you make you will be judged, and the measure you give will be the measure you get. Why do you see the speck in your neighbour's eye, but do not notice the log in your own eye?

Or how can you say to your neighbour, "let me take the speck out of your eye?" You hypocrite first take the log out of your own eye, and then you will see clearly to take the speck out of your neighbour's eye.

Now let's get to the celebrations. There are so many outstanding books out there that help to outline "the best wedding" format. If you have chosen the Event Planner route, great! Some event planners are amazing and take the worry off your shoulders for that big day. In my references, I have listed several I have worked with and some I hope to work with.

For the wedding ceremony, the officiant is the one that helps make the ceremony happen. Without a wedding officiant, it is just a party. Like most professionals, you pay for what you get. Sometime the cheapest isn't the best nor is the most expensive. As with all the other vendors you will hire for this special day, the three of you need to have a connection.

When looking to hire an officiant, please check with Ontario Services on-line that they are registered and therefore have the authority to sign the marriage licence and that they have a blue marriage registry.

As a note, the Ontario Services site is not a mobile friendly site and using a computer will accurately show the list with details such as names, congregation, location and registration number.

This is important. I had a couple who had a friend from the USA, perform and sign their marriage licence, only to discover that he wasn't registered here in Canada. I tried to help by performing another wedding ceremony, and then we signed the forms again. That did not help either, as once completed improperly the

Registered Office will not accept it. So please make sure your officiants are registered (and that they do have a certificate as well). Don't just take their word for it.

If you choose me as your officiant, this is how we move forward.

We meet to see if we are a suitable fit.

Our first meeting may be a video chat or meeting in person to see if we could work well together. I will ask you questions like:

- Tell me about your Love story
- How long have you been seeing each other?
- Have you been to other weddings lately?
- What parts of these wedding ceremonies did you like or dislike?
- How much thought have you put into your wedding ceremony?

Then you most likely have a ton of questions you would like to ask me, such as, "What are my fees?", "How long have I been doing this?" and more. I will answer most of these questions in Chapter Three.

I so enjoy hearing how couples met and what their first dates were like. Their synchronicity always intrigues me. I know now that about 80 percent of my couples find each other online. Be it swiping left or right, you were brave enough to look for a relationship beyond just waiting at home for the doorbell to ring, "Here I am."

On October 17, 2017, I read an article by Drake Baer, on LinkedIn, "How Online Dating is Creating Stronger Marriages." Here is what I took from his piece:

- You are pushed beyond your social circle
- 1 out 3 marriages in America today happens between people who met online
- Tinder alone produces 26 million matches a day
- There is a boom in interracial marriages
- It pulls people outside of their network. This means they can find better personality compatibility with potential partners.
- Marriages created after online dating occurs are better because online dating gives you more choices while searching for a partner.
- It's like going to a large party and finding someone who is interested in you

These are just a few experiences of how couples have met each other:

I remember one young couple in their early twenties who met on Tinder. They made their first meeting at a coffee shop in the middle of town to be feel safe and around people. She was very nervous because he was the cutest guy she had ever met and he turned out to be just as nervous as she was because he found her to be so adorable. Their love was genuine, and the wedding ceremony was as if I was marrying Prince Charming and Cinderella. So much compassion and patience with each other.

Then there was the couple in their thirties who met at a bar via a total stranger who said, "I believe that man is waiting for you," to her and, "I believe that lady is waiting for you", to him. And then when they both turned around to identify him to each other, he disappeared. One special match maker!

Another couple, in their forties, had both been married before. The man was a widower and when he met his new bride-to-be through mutual friends, he knew she was the one on their first meeting at a friends' place and so did she. They just got that feeling and needed to explore it more.

And I have had a few who were friends since they were kids but didn't pay attention to each other. Then as they grew up and came back from university everything just fell into the right places and they acknowledged their newfound love for each other.

We Move to the Next Steps

First Form and Financial Information

After the call, I will forward my complete list of fees, in case I haven't already sent them to you and a form called "The Next Steps". This form is required if you want to hire me. Details are found in the Appendix section. This outlines requirements such as requesting your full names, addresses, phones to be used on the day of ceremony (just in case I am required to contact you before I arrive), which package you have chosen and how you will submit the retainer. If you postpone your wedding, we will find a date and time that will accommodate.

Note: If you cancel the wedding, the retainer is non-refundable, but you can apply it to other professional services that I provide i.e. Energy Healing. You can find more details regarding my healing practice on my website, www.marymontanari.com. Here I provide a full description of my services to connect you to your inner peace via energy healing, past life regression or even meditation.

Upon receiving the retainer, I will send you a receipt with all the details provided in the completed "The Next Steps" form.

You Craft Your Ceremony!

Then I ask the couple to review the vows and readings provided in this book to create your wedding ceremony. Once you send me your selection or other personal favorites, I will start to create the ceremony and email the draft for your review.

We may want to meet up face-to-face a month or two before the wedding to see how your event planning is progressing. I enjoy these moments as it gives us a chance to get to know each other even more. Time permitting, of course.

Chapter Three
FREQUENTLY ASKED QUESTIONS

My partner and I are on a budget. What's the most economical package you offer?

The Elopement package is the most economical and, no, this just doesn't mean running away to get married. This package is the most basic one I offer for $200.00 during this publication year, 2020. It includes a brief ceremony, which covers the completion of all the legal terms, and you bring the rings, the two of you and your two witnesses. Once the "I do's" have been exchanged the legal documents are completed. If you don't have witnesses, I can hire two people to be your witnesses for an extra $50.00. No extra guests for this package. Short and sweet. Very cost efficient.

We want our best friend to conduct our wedding ceremony. Can you work with them?

I'm a team player and my purpose is to ensure the ceremony is exactly what the two of you want. My role can be as simple as standing on the side and stepping in to perform the official part of the ceremony, and after you sign the papers, your friend can introduce you as a married couple to your guests. Or, I can be part of creating the ceremony, running the rehearsal, and then stand next to your friend during the ceremony. Another option is that I either arrive earlier or after, to get the legal papers signed. It all depends how involved you require my services to be and the price reflects this

We're getting married outside of the GTA. Are you willing to travel?

Absolutely! For weddings outside of the GTA, my fee includes travel time. If online consultation isn't enough and you also need a rehearsal, I charge for my travel time. The fee is usually $150.00-$180.00, depending on how much travel is needed or if accommodations are required. These are issues that need to be discussed with each couple personally.

Who's responsible for getting the marriage licence?

You are. Visit the Government of Ontario website (Service Ontario) to find out how to get a marriage licence. You can download and print the form and take it to an Office of Registrar closest to you. Once I've performed your ceremony, I'll mail your signed marriage licence to Service Ontario to register it. Twelve weeks after that you can order a copy of your marriage certificate from the same site.

Note: I always tell my couples that they can apply right after the ceremony on-line, to help speed up the process.

We are having a destination wedding and need forms completed. Can you help?

For sure. Get the marriage licence, and then we have some options, either a quick paper signing with two witnesses at an agreed upon meeting place or we can meet at a local restaurant, café, or even a park to get the signing done.

How can we get the Marriage Certificate as soon as possible?

First, we need to complete some paperwork before we mail the Marriage Licence to Office of the Registrar General.

You will need to get a Marriage Licence as discussed above.

Then go on-line to Service Ontario to apply for the Marriage Certificate, even though we have not completed the Marriage Licence yet. The Office will issue you a registration number once you have paid for the certificate.

You will need to write a note to The Registrar General, detailing the urgency of this request. Include the Marriage Licence number and the registration number of the Marriage Certificate.

Purchase a prepaid Canada Priority Envelope at the Post Office

The day of ceremony you will have: Marriage Licence, registration number from Marriage Certificate application, Letter to Registrar General, prepaid envelope, and 2 witnesses.

We will then perform the ceremony with your two witnesses and complete the marriage licence. Take a photo for your records and we put everything in the Canada Priority Envelope addressed to the Office of the Registrar General, and then the Officiant will mail it ASAP.

We have changed our minds, and the wedding is off. Can we get our money back?

Unfortunately, the answer is no. The time you had requested was reserved, recorded with my affiliation and prevents any other weddings to be booked for that day and time. This payment covers the time the Officiant has taken when discussing your wedding plans, customized and created your ceremony.

What I have allowed is that you can use the funds for another service that I provide as an energy healer and teacher.

Do you stay for the reception and dinner after the ceremony?

Most venues charge by the plate for the reception and guest lists are limited at times. I prefer to stay a bit after the ceremony, if permitted, to toast with your family and then quietly find the door to leave.

There have been a few weddings, though, where I was asked to attend the reception after the ceremony to help with prayers before the meal and just be part of the family celebration that we had all worked so hard to create.

My mom, dad, grandparent, or another family member dear to us has passed way recently. What would you suggest we do to honour them?

My prayers are with you all during a time where you really wanted them around to celebrate with you. Love never dies, but the missing them seems to linger. That love lives with us, always, so why not create areas in the venue to honour their memory:

A. At the signing in table have frames filled with family photos. It is beautiful to place old photos of all your married grandparents and even of your own parents. Note: in divorce situations, it will be up to the couple whether they feel comfortable with this form of remembrance. Sometimes in divorce many people forget that they did marry for a reason and sometimes life changes.

B. Placing a photo of the deceased loved one on a chair with flowers or placing the framed photo on the signing table next to the bride's bouquet.

C. Using granddad's handkerchief that day to help wipe the tears of the bride or groom during the ceremony.

D. Covering the signing table with a family heirloom tablecloth or toasting with the family crystal or silver glasses.

Chapter Four

CHOOSING YOUR VOWS

It's time to cuddle up with your partner and experience the power of love through words. Keep in mind that all may be interchanged for your needs or used to create your own personal vows.

Many couples now like to write their own individual vows filled with their promises, likes, dislikes, and a few personal comments. I like to provide my couples with some samples if they get lost with their words and need a few. The key point is to write from the heart. Take a few minutes to let yourself remember those special things you love about them. Sometime the words just follow naturally and sometimes they need inspiration like:

- What is it that makes you feel alive with your partner?
- Maybe think about a full day you spent together and what you loved about it.
- How do you travel together?
- Share a funny story and how it has made you a better person

- Will you be comfortable to share these vows with others as you stand together?
- How long do you want to make your vows: short and sweet or full of details?

If this is a second marriage with children, perhaps you'd like to include them in your vows. I have had weddings where the couple read their own vows as commitments to each other and then separate ones for the children. Another couple consolidated the vows as "the New Family Promises."

The cutest moment was one serious, quiet groom informed me that he wrote his vows but needed help, so he stole a few ideas from my samples. "Will that be ok?" Of course, it is!

Another couple spent several days creating their own vows. They separately emailed me a week before the walk through. I prepared their vows on pretty stationary and they read them silently to themselves as we were getting ready for the practice. All went well, till the day of the wedding the couple got so nervous about reading in front of their family that they opted out and we did the simple one where I just ask the questions. I suggested that they can always read them during the honeymoon when no one else is around. They loved that idea!!

Note: all these vows maybe interchanged with titles i.e. bride and bride, groom and groom, they and they.

Sample vows

SIMPLE

This one is great to use if you want a short and simple ceremony. It's also helpful if you don't want to stand in front of your guests for a long time with tears in your eyes.

Officiant:
(Turning to the groom)

_____ you have chosen _____to be your wife. Will you love and respect her? Will you be honest with her always? Will you stand by her through whatever may come? (Answer "I do" or "I will")

Then the Officiant asks the bride:

_____, you have chosen _____ to be your husband. Will you love and respect him? Will you be honest with him always? Will you stand by him through whatever may come? (Answer "I will" or "I do")

FROM THE BOOK OF COMMON PRAYER

First, the groom makes his vows:

I _____ take thee _____ to be my wedded Wife, to have and to hold from this day forward, for better for worse, for richer, for poorer, in sickness and in health, to love and to cherish, till death us do us part, according to God's holy ordinance; and thereto I plight thee my troth.

With this Ring I thee wed: In the Name of the Father, and of the Son, and of the Holy Ghost. Amen.

Then the bride makes her vows:

I _____ take thee _____to be my wedded husband to have and to hold from this day forward, for better, for worse, for richer, for poorer, in sickness and in health, to love and to cherish, till death us do us part, according to God's holy ordinance; and there to I plight thee my troth.

With this Ring I thee wed: In the Name of the Father, and of the Son, and of the Holy Ghost. Amen.

ROMAN CATHOLIC

Use these if you want to keep family Roman Catholic traditions.

Officiant to the groom:

_____, please place _____'s ring upon the third finger of her left hand and recite your vows after me:

I, _____, take you _____ to be my wife,

I promise to be true to you in good times and in bad, in sickness and in health.

I will love you and honor you all the days of my life.

_____, take this ring as a sign of my love and fidelity in the name of the Father, and of the Son and of the Holy Spirit.

Officiant to the bride:

_____, please place _____'s ring upon the third finger of his left hand and recite your vows after me:

I, _____, take you _____ to be my husband,

I promise to be true to you in good times and in bad, in sickness and in health.

I will love you and honor you all the days of my life.

_____ take this ring as a sign of my love and fidelity in the name of the Father, and of the Son and of the Holy Spirit.

EPISCOPAL

In the Name of God, I, _____, take you, _____, to be my wife, to have and to hold from this day forward, for better, for worse, for richer, for poorer, in sickness and in health, to love and to cherish until we are parted by death. This is my solemn vow.

In the Name of God, I, _____, take you _____ to be my husband, to have and to hold from this day forward, for better, for worse, for richer, for poorer, in sickness and in health, to love and to cherish until we are parted by death. This is my solemn vow.

UNITARIAN

I, _____, take you, _____, to be the wife of my days, to be the parent of my children, to be the companion of my house. We will keep together what measure of trouble and sorrow our lives may lay upon us, and we will share together our store of goodness and plenty and love.

I, _____ take you, _____, to be the husband of my days, to be the parent of my children, to be the companion of my house. We will keep together what measure of trouble and sorrow our lives may lay upon us, and we will share together our store of goodness and plenty and love.

JEWISH

Note: we can always have a friend or family member say the parts in Hebrew beside the Officiant to add a personal touch.

Harei at m'kudeshet li b'taba'at zo kedat Moshe v'Yisrael. Behold, you are consecrated to me with this ring according to the laws of Moses and Israel.

V'erastikh li l'olam, v'erastikh li b'tzedek uvmishpat uv'chesed uv'rachamim V'erastikh li b'emunah v'yada'at et Adonai.

I betroth you to myself forever; I betroth you to myself in righteousness and in justice, in love and in mercy; I betroth you to myself in faithfulness, and you shall know G-d

THE PROTESTANT WEDDING SOURCEBOOK

In the presence of God and before our family and friends,

I, _____, take you, _____, to be my wife. All that I am I give to you, and all that I have I share with you. Whatever the future holds, I will love you and stand by you, as long as we both shall live. This is my solemn vow.

In the presence of God and before our family and friends, I, _____, take you, _____, to be my husband. All that I am I give to you, and all that I have I share with you. Whatever the future holds, I will love you and stand by you, as long as we both shall live. This is my solemn vow.

QUAKER

In the presence of God and these our Friends, I take thee to be my wife, promising with Divine assistance to be unto thee a loving and faithful husband so long as we both shall live.

In the presence of God and these our Friends, I take thee to be my husband, promising with Divine assistance to be unto thee a loving and faithful wife so long as we both shall live.

CHURCH OF ENGLAND

This is called the Anglican Church in Canada.

The groom vows:

I _____, take you _____, to be my wife

to have and to hold
from this day forward;
for better, for worse,
for richer, for poorer,
in sickness and in health,
to love and to cherish,
till death us do part,
according to God's holy law;
in the presence of God I make this vow.

The bride vows:

I _____ take you _____, to be my husband,
to have and to hold
from this day forward;
for better, for worse,
for richer, for poorer,
in sickness and in health,
to love and to cherish,
till death us do part,
according to God's holy law;
in the presence of God I make this vow.

TRADITIONAL SECULAR VOWS

The groom vows:

I, _____, commit myself to you, _____, as husband to learn and grow with, to explore and adventure with, to respect you in everything as an equal partner, in the foreknowledge of joy and pain, strength and weariness, direction and doubt, for all the risings and settings of the sun. We tie these knots to symbolize our connection to one another. They represent our trust in each other and our combined strength together.

Then the bride vows:

I, _____, commit myself to you, _____, as wife to learn and grow with, to explore and adventure with, to respect you in everything as an equal partner, in the foreknowledge of joy and pain, strength and weariness, direction and doubt, for all the risings and settings of the sun. We tie these knots to symbolize our connection to one another. They represent our trust in each other and our combined strength together.

* * *

Alternate version I:

The groom vows:

Today, surrounded by people who love us, I choose you _____ to be my partner. I am proud to be your husband and to join my life with yours. I vow to support you, push you, inspire you, and above all love you, for better or worse, in sickness and health, for richer or poorer, as long as we both shall live

Then the bride vows:

Today, surrounded by people who love us, I choose you _____ to be my partner. I am proud to be your wife and to join my life with yours. I vow to support you, push you, inspire you, and above all love you, for better or worse, in sickness and health, for richer or poorer, as long as we both shall live.

* * *

Alternate version II:

Another style is that the couple answers "We do" afte

OFFICIANT: _____ and _____, if you will face each other and repeat after me:

_____, I give you my life. With all that I am and all that I have, I honor you.

_____, I give you my life. With all that I am and all that I have, I honor you.

* * *

Alternate version III:

First the groom vows:

I, _____, take you _____ to be the wife of my days, the companion of my house, the friend of my life. We shall bear together whatever trouble and sorrow life may lay upon us, and we shall share together whatever good and joyful things life may bring us. With these words, and all the words of my heart, I marry you and bind my life to yours.

Then the bride vows:

I, _____, take you _____ to be the husband of my days, the companion of my house, the friend of my life. We shall bear together whatever trouble and sorrow life may lay upon us, and we shall share together whatever good and joyful things life may bring us. With these words, and all the words of my heart, I marry you and bind my life to yours.

* * *

Alternate version IV:

You have taught me that two people joined together with respect, trust, and open communication can be far stronger and happier than each could ever be alone. You are the strength I didn't know I needed, and the joy that I didn't know I lacked. Today, I choose to spend the rest of my life with you. I promise to love you for who you are, and for who you are yet to become. I promise to be patient, and to remember that all things between us are rooted in love. I promise to nurture your dreams and to help you reach them. I promise to share my whole heart with you, and to remember to show you how deeply I care for you, no matter the challenges that may come our way. I promise to love you loyally and fiercely—as long as I shall live.

Do you take me to be your lawfully wedded [husband/wife]?

* * *

Alternate version V:

I, _____, do pledge you, _____, my love, for as long as I live. What I possess in this world, I give to you. I will keep you and hold you, comfort and tend you, protect you and shelter you, for all the days of my life.

I, _____, do pledge you, _____, my love, for as long as I live. What I possess in this world, I give to you. I will keep you and hold you, comfort and tend you, protect you and shelter you, for all the days of my life.

Alternate version VI:

These are fun as you say them together.

OFFICIANT: Do you, _____ and _____ pledge to create a life of mutual respect, compassion, generosity, and patience toward each other as you grow together in years?

COUPLE: We do.

OFFICIANT: Do you pledge to recognize each other's individuality and celebrate each other's uniqueness as a strength in marriage. While at the same time, will you guard one another's weaknesses with understanding, support, and inspiration?

COUPLE: We do.

OFFICIANT: And do you pledge to share the love you have for each other with all living beings? To be a couple that lets their marriage radiate into others, making their lives more beautiful because of it?

Note: this may be added to any of the vows:
Most of all, I promise to help you have compassion for yourself, so that you can thrive and be happy.

Alternate version VII:

The first person vows:

_____, please repeat after me:

I, _____, pledge to you_____
A life of giving and hoping
A life of growing and loving
I shall share with you
Both my work and my play
I shall be with you
In your tears and in your laughter
Just as I will bring my own sorrows
And my own joys to you
I accept you as my companion
And pledge to your honor, faith and love

The second person vows:

_____, please repeat after me:

I, _____, pledge to you_____
A life of giving and hoping
A life of growing and loving
I shall share with you
Both my work and my play
I shall be with you
In your tears and in your laughter
Just as I will bring my own sorrows
And my own joys to you
I accept you as my companion
And pledge to your honor, faith and love.

Chapter Five
READING POETRY TOGETHER

This section contains a selection of verse from well-known authors and sacred texts.

Corinthians 13:4-7, English Standard Version

Love is always patient and kind. It is never jealous. Love is never boastful or conceited, it is never rude or selfish, it does not take offense and is not resentful. Love takes no pleasure in other people's faults but delights in the truth. It is always ready to excuse, to trust, to hope. It is always ready to endure whatever comes. True love does not come to an end.

Buddha

Live in joy, In Love,
Even among those who hate.

Live in joy, In health,
Even among the afflicted.

Live in joy, In peace,
Even among the troubled.

The Good-Morrow, by John Donne

I wonder, by my troth, what thou and I
Did, till we loved? Were we not weaned till then?
But sucked on country pleasures, childishly?
Or snorted we in the Seven Sleepers' den?
'Twas so; but this, all pleasures fancies be.
If ever any beauty I did see,
Which I desired, and got, 'twas but a dream of thee.

And now good-morrow to our waking souls,
Which watch not one another out of fear;
For love, all love of other sights controls,
And makes one little room an everywhere.
Let sea-discoverers to new worlds have gone,
Let maps to other, worlds on worlds have shown,
Let us possess one world, each hath one, and is one.

My face in thine eye, thine in mine appears,
And true plain hearts do in the faces rest;
Where can we find two better hemispheres,
Without sharp north, without declining west?
Whatever dies, was not mixed equally;
If our two loves be one, or, thou and I
Love so alike, that none do slacken, none can die.

Invitation to Love, by Paul Lawrence Dunbar

Come when the nights are bright with stars
Or come when the moon is mellow;
Come when the sun his golden bars
Drops on the hay-field yellow.
Come in the twilight soft and gray,

Come in the night or come in the day,
Come, O love, whene'er you may,
And you are welcome, welcome.

You are sweet, O Love, dear Love,
You are soft as the nesting dove.
Come to my heart and bring it to rest
As the bird flies home to its welcome nest.

Come when my heart is full of grief
Or when my heart is merry;
Come with the falling of the leaf
Or with the redd'ning cherry.
Come when the year's first blossom blows,
Come when the summer gleams and glows,
Come with the winter's drifting snows,
And you are welcome, welcome.

Kahlil Gibran

Let there be spaces in your togetherness,
And let the winds of the heavens dance between you.
Love one another but make not a bond of love: Let it rather be a moving sea between the shores of your souls.
Fill each other's cup but drink not from one cup.
Give one another of your bread but eat not from the same loaf.
Sing and dance together and be joyous, but let each one of you be alone,
Even as the strings of a lute are alone though they quiver with the same music.
Give your hearts, but not into each other's keeping. For only the hand of Life can contain your hearts.

And stand together, yet not too near together:
For the pillars of the temple stand apart, And the oak tree and the cypress grow not in each other's shadow.

Thoughts on Marriage from *The Prophet,* by Kahlil Gibran

You were born together, and together you shall be forever more.
You shall be together when the white wings of death scatter your days.
Yes, you shall be together even in the silent memory of God.
But let there be spaces in your togetherness.
And let the winds of heaven dance between you.
Love one another, but make not a bond of love.
Let it rather be a moving sea between the shores of your souls.
Fill each other's cup but drink not from one cup.
Give one another of your bread but eat not from the same loaf.
Sing and dance together and be joyous, but each one of you be alone--even as the strings of a lute are alone though the quiver with the same music.
Give your hearts, but not in each other's keeping.
For only the hand of Life can contain your hearts.
And stand together yet not too near together:
For the pillars of the temple stand apart,
And the oak tree and the Cyprus grow not in each other's shadows

Mark 10:6-9

But from the beginning of creation, God made them male and female. For this reason a man shall leave his father and mother and be joined to his wife, and the two shall become one flesh. So they are no longer two, but one flesh. Therefore what God has joined together, let no one separate."

Maybe, by Author Unknown

Maybe....we are supposed to meet the wrong people before we meet the right one so when they finally arrive we are truly grateful for the gift we have been given.

Maybe....it's true that we don't know what we have lost until we lose it but it is also true that we don't know what we're missing until it arrives.

Maybe....the happiest of people don't have the best of everything but make the best of everything that comes their way.

Maybe....the best kind of love is the kind where you sit on the sofa together, not saying a word and walk away feeling like it was the best conversation you've ever had.

Maybe....once in a lifetime you find someone who not only touches your heart but also your soul, someone who loves you for who you are and not what you could be.

Maybe...the art of true love is not about finding the perfect person, but about seeing an imperfect person perfectly.

Wedding Hymn, by Sidney Lanier

Thou God, whose high, eternal Love
Is the only blue sky of our life,
Clear all the Heaven that bends above
The life-road of this man and wife.
May these two lives be but one note
In the world's strange-sounding harmony,
Whose sacred music e'er shall float
Through every discord up to Thee.

As when from separate stars two beams
Unite to form one tender ray:
As when two sweet but shadowy dreams
Explain each other in the day:
So may these two dear hearts one light
Emit, and each interpret each.
Let an angel come and dwell tonight
In this dear double-heart, and teach.

The One, by Author Unknown

When the one whose hand you're holding is the one who holds your heart, When the one whose eyes you gaze into gives your hopes and dreams their start, When the one you think of first and last is the one who holds you tight, And the things you plan together makes the whole world seem just right, When the one whom you believe in puts their faith and trust in you, You've found the one and only to share your whole life through.

Short Poem from Rumi

And of everything
We have created pairs.
Heaven and Earth
Night and Day
Sun and Moon
Shore and Sea
Light and Darkness
Her,
For Him

The Most Alive Moment, by Rumi

The most living moment comes when those
who love each other meet each other's eyes
and in what flows between them then.
To see your face in a crowd of others,
or alone on a frightening street,
I weep for that.
Our tears improve the earth.
The time you scolded me, your gratitude,
your laughing,
always your qualities increase the soul.
Seeing you
is a wine that does not muddle or numb.

We sit inside the cypress shadow
where amazement and clear thought
twine its growth into it.

A Blessing from Rumi

May these vows and this marriage be blessed.
May it be sweet milk,
this marriage, like wine and halvah.
May this marriage offer fruit and shade, like the date palm.
May this marriage be full of laughter,
our every day a paradise.
May this marriage be a sign of compassion,
a seal of happiness here and hereafter.
May this marriage have a fair face and a good name,
an omen as welcome

as the moon in a clear blue sky.
I am out of words to describe
how spirit mingles in this marriage.

Privileged Lovers, by Rumi

The moon has become a dancer
at this festival of love.
This dance of light,
This sacred blessing,
This divine love,
beckons us
to a world beyond
only lovers can see
with their eyes of fiery passion.
They are the chosen ones
who have surrendered.
Once they were particles of light
now they are the radiant sun.
They have left behind
the world of deceitful games.
They are the privileged lovers
who create a new world
with their eyes of fiery passion.

Sonnet 116: Let me not to the marriage of true minds, by William Shakespeare

Let me not to the marriage of true minds
Admit impediments. Love is not love
Which alters when it alteration finds,
Or bends with the remover to remove.
O no! it is an ever-fixed mark

That looks on tempests and is never shaken;
It is the star to every wand'ring bark,
Whose worth's unknown, although his height be taken.
Love's not Time's fool, though rosy lips and cheeks
Within his bending sickle's compass come;
Love alters not with his brief hours and weeks,
But bears it out even to the edge of doom.
If this be error and upon me prov'd,
I never writ, nor no man ever lov'd.

A Poem by Mark Twain

A marriage makes of two fractional lives a whole;
It gives two purposeless lives a work,
And doubles the strength of each to perform it.
It gives to two questioning natures a reason for living
And something to live for.
It will give new gladness to the sunshine,
A new fragrance to the flowers, a new beauty to the earth
And a new mystery to life.

Excerpt from "The Velveteen Rabbit", by Margery Williams

"What is REAL?" asked the Rabbit one day, when they were lying side by side near the nursery fender. "Does it mean having things that buzz inside you and a stick-out handle?"

"Real isn't how you are made," said the Skin Horse. "It's a thing that happens to you.

When a child loves you for a long, long time, not just to play with, but **Really** loves you, then you become **Real**."

"Does it hurt?" asked the Rabbit.

"Sometimes," said the Skin Horse, for he was always truthful. "When you are Real you don't mind being hurt."

"Does it happen all at once, like being wound up," he asked, "or bit by bit?"

"It doesn't happen all at once," said the Skin Horse. "You become. It takes a long time. That's why it doesn't happen often to people who break easily, or have sharp edges, or who have to be carefully kept. Generally, by the time you are Real, most of your hair has been loved off, and your eyes drop out and you get all loose in the joints and very shabby. But these things don't matter at all, because once you are Real you can't be ugly, except to people who don't understand."

Chapter Six

MY MOST POPULAR TRADITIONAL AND FAMILY CEREMONIES

These are some of my own personal wedding ceremony highlights and unique ceremonies.

One can deepen their knowledge by researching the internet and crafting their own.

Keep in mind that all roles can be interchanged with important family members or friends.

I love learning and I'm always delighted to experience another new cultural practise. The following are the most popular ceremonies I have performed. There are still more to experience and thank goodness for Google!

Same sex marriage

Excerpt from a groom and groom wedding.

They chose this particular reading:

By Kavanaugh….. slightly modified

To love is not to possess,
To own or imprison,
Nor to lose one's self in another.
Love is to join and separate,
To walk alone and together,

It is finally to be able
To be who we really are.
It is to be perfectly one's self
And perfectly joined in permanent commitment
To another.

Love only endures when it moves like waves,
Receding and returning gently or passionately,
Or moving lovingly like the tide
In the moon's own predictable harmony,
Because finally,
They are openly free to be
Who they really are--and always secretly were,
In the very core of their being
Where true and lasting love can alone abide.

Vow and the Expression of Intent and Consent

In acknowledging your intent _____ and _____, I am required to ask your intent.

_____ first.

_____, you have chosen _____ to be your husband. Will you love and respect him? Will you be honest with him always? Will you stand by him through whatever may come? (Answer "I will", or "I do")

Put ring on _____'s hand.

_____, you have chosen _____ to be your husband. Will you love and respect him? Will you be honest with him always? Will you stand by him through whatever may come? (Answer "I will", or "I do")

Puts ring on _____'s hand.

Declaration of Marriage

_____ and _____, your lives and spirits are joined in a union of love and trust. Your love should be a constant source of light, and like the earth, a firm foundation from which to grow. As you have consented in this ceremony in the presence of friends and family to be partners for life, I now pronounce you spiritually united and bound together body and soul. It is with great joy and privilege by the virtue of the powers vested in me, to hereby pronounce you husband and husband.

You may kiss each other.

Parts from a Renewal of Wedding Vows on a 10th Anniversary with a Family Gem Ceremony

Keep in mind that a gem ceremony can be replaced with sand, water or another precious metal that best represents the couple or family involved.

Vow and the Expression of Intent and Consent

Now, to recognize your intent in this cordial setting. First for you _____.

_____, ____ years ago, you chose _____ **to** be your wife. And, _____ told me Do you continue to love and respect her? Will you be honest with her always? Will you continue to stand by her through whatever may come?

(Answer "I will")

_____, ____ years ago, you chose _____ to be your husband. Do you continue to love and respect him? Will you be honest with him always? Will you continue to stand by him through whatever may come?

(Answer "I will")

Now for _____ and_____, do you pledge to move forward with a renewed commitment to each other?

(Answer "We Do").

Do you pledge that from this day forward you will be each other's number one priority?

(Answer "We Do").

Do you promise to be together in a partnership for all that life brings your way?

(Answer "We Do").

Do you promise to do this while having fun, laughing and enjoying your family together?

(Answer "Always!").

Put ring on _____'s hand.

Puts ring on _____'s hand.

They Chose, Marriage Joins Two People, by Edmund O'Neil

Marriage offers opportunities for sharing growth
that no other human relationship can equal.
It is an emotional and physical joining that is promised for a lifetime.
Within the circle of love,
marriage encompasses all of life's most important relationships.
A wife and husband are each other's best friend,
confidant, lover, teacher, listener and critic.
Marriage deepens and enriches every facet of life.
Happiness is fuller; memories are fresher;
even anger is felt more intensely and passes away more quickly.
Marriage understands and forgives,
the mistakes that life is unavoidable to avoid.
It encourages and nurtures new life, new experiences
and new ways of expressing your love through the seasons.
When two people pledge to love and care for each other in marriage,
they create a spirit unique to themselves,
which binds them closer than any spoken or written words.
Marriage is a promise and potential,

made in the hearts of two people who are in love, that takes a lifetime to fulfill.

One devoted couple chose a gem ceremony for their 2 beautiful daughters, ages 7 and 5 years old to be a part of. For me, the best part of this was arriving early and listening to those two girls describing to their cousins what they were going to be doing with these pretty, different-coloured, plastic shaped gems as they were all standing around the table with just their heads peering out. The amazing part was during the part of the ceremony when the gem pouring took place, all the kids watched in silence. Once the ceremony was completed, they retold the story to their parents describing why the family decided to perform it and who chose which colour, shape and why. Emphasizing the importance of educating and involving children in any form of wedding ceremony is beneficial for all.

Gem Stone Ceremony

_____ and _____

And will _____ and _____

Come and join us at the table

On the table there will be four individual containers filled with gems for each member of the family.

I ask each one of you to pick up their container that represents them. Each one of you is holding your own personal gems which represents your uniqueness.

Now let us gradually pour each one into the larger container that now represents the family. Put together you are whole with your unique parts.

I emphasize that each of you is special and your independence can still show through even when together which makes it even better as a whole.

Declaration of Marriage

_____ and _____, having witnessed your renewed vows for marriage with all who are assembled here, it is with great joy and privilege by the virtue of the powers vested in me, to hereby pronounce you husband and wife. Again. You may seal your vow with a kiss.

_____, you may kiss your beautiful bride.

Water Ceremony

The couple have chosen a Water ceremony to express their connection with each other and life. One couple that chose this ceremony reminded me of Robin Hood and Maid Marian. Their venue was at a conservation area north of Toronto and the backdrop was a luscious green wooded forest.

We walked over to a vintage solid oak table that had the plant and separate watering containers. There will be containers on the table with a pretty plant, and two smaller vases with water in them. You will both take one smaller container each and as I say the prayer you start to pour together in the larger one.

Prayer:
Nothing in the world is softer and weaker than water.

But for attacking the hard, the unyielding, nothing can surpass it.

There is nothing like it.

_____ and _____ have chosen water to be their symbol of their love, individual but together stronger and inseparable.

Handfasting Ceremony

This is a Celtic tradition that goes back over 2000 years. A druid priest wrapped a rope, vine, or scarf on the hands of the couple declared them bound together. It can easily be explained as the binding together of their separate lives and the promises they're making together. If you want a ceremony where you get friends and family members involved this is a great one! The more people we get involved the more promises are shared.

Here is an example where my couple had their siblings and friends come up and place a ribbon for each promise. The colours of the ribbons were all matching and about two meters in length so that they fell gracefully around the couple's hands. It was ideal for photographs.

Officiant:
The First Promise
_____, will you be _____'s faithful partner for life?

_____, says, "I WILL."

_____, will you be _____'s faithful partner for life?

_____ says, "I WILL."

Officiant:
Will you be each other's constant friends and one true love?

_____ and _____ say, "WE WILL."

First cord is draped across _____ and _____'s hands and so the first binding is made.

Officiant:
The Second Promise

_____, do you promise to love _____ without reservation?

_____ says, "I WILL."

_____, do you promise to love _____ without reservation?

_____ says, "I WILL."

Officiant:
Will both of you stand by one another in sickness and in health, in plenty and in want?

_____ and _____ say, "WE WILL."

Second cord is draped across _____ and _____'s hands and so the second binding is made.

Officiant:
The Third Promise

_____, will you stand together with _____ your times of joy and sorrow?

_____ says, "I WILL."

_____, will you stand together with _____ your times of joy and sorrow?

_____ says, "I WILL."

Officiant:

Will you share the burdens of each so that your spirits may grow in this union?

_____ and _____ say, "WE WILL."

Third cord is draped across _____ and _____'s hands and so the third binding is made.

Officiant:
The Forth Promise

_____, will you always be open and honest with _____, for as long as you both shall live?

_____ says, "I WILL."

_____, will you always be open and honest with _____, for as long as you both shall live?

_____ says, "I WILL."

Officiant:
Will you dream together to create new realities and hopes for this marriage?

_____ and _____ say, "WE WILL."

Fourth cord is draped across _____ and _____'s hands and so the fourth binding is made.

Officiant:
The Fifth Promise

_____, Will you honour this man?

_____ says, "I WILL."

_____, Will you honour this woman?

Groom says, "I Will."

Officiant:
Will you both seek to cherish and strengthen that honour?

_____ and _____ say, "WE WILL."

Fifth cord is draped across _____ and _____'s hands and so the fifth binding is made.

Officiant:
Binding of all promises

The knots of these bindings are not formed by these cords but instead by your vows. Either of you may drop the cords, for as always, you hold in your own hands the making or breaking of this union.

Officiant then may add:
These ribbons will be removed and placed on the honeymoon door to indicate do not disturb!

The cords are removed and placed on table.

Korean Tradition of the Jeonanrye Ceremony

Please note that in this ceremony the couple chose the duck instead of the geese. There is no right or wrong. Just their personal preference and what they could find at the time.

The Jeonanrye ceremony consists of a kireogi or of two wooden geese. The wild goose is a symbol of harmony, structure and a mate for life. The groom bows twice before presenting the kireogi to his future mother-in-law. The groom is promising a life of love and care to the woman's daughter. Note: wild geese understand hierarchy and order. Even when flying, they maintain structure and harmony. Once the vows have been exchanged, the mother of the bride offers wine from a cup or traditional carved out gourd. The bride and groom walk over and bow before they accept the wine.

In November of 2018, the couple and I designed this ceremony to adjust to their style.

The groom made 1,000 white paper cranes by hand (which he brought with him from the USA in his carry-on luggage) and then constructed a copper piping frame here in Toronto to display them! For him, the cranes represented fidelity, longevity and a successful marriage. They chose to have this as their backdrop during the ceremony.

Officiant:

Traditional ceremony

Korean tradition is to honour the mother of the bride with either a goose or a wooden duck, as a symbol of harmony and structure. Mandarin duck mates for life, so by giving the mother a duck, the groom is promising a life of love and care to the woman's daughter.

_____ and _____ walk over to get the ducks.

Then walk first to _____'s mother, hand her a duck and then bow and hug!

Then walk to _____'s mother, hand her a duck and then bow and hug!

Chinese Tea Ceremony

This can be performed either on the day of the wedding or a few days before, it all depends on the timing with the elders and the venue. I love this ceremony as family are honoured and the tea ceremony has always been a part of my own personal practice.

Each area of Asia has its own receipt for the tea. One recipe: black tea, red dates, peanuts, longans, and lotus seeds. The

Chinese say the reason the words are in this order is "to have baby as soon as possible".

What is the significance of this ceremony?

The bride and groom pay their respects and show gratitude towards their families, who in turn bless the newlyweds as they start their life as husband and wife.

They officially belong into a new, extended family. During the ceremony, the bride and groom will address the relatives with their new titles while serving them tea.

What do you need to prepare for the ceremony?

1. Two red cushions to kneel on - one for the groom and one for the bride.
2. The Chinese tea as described above with possibly even a pu'er tieguanyin or jasmine tea as the base. The tea set requires enough cups for all of the family members. There are also some really pretty paper ones that can be purchased and make the ceremony run smoother if there are a lot of members to serve.
3. Basket in which to place red envelopes and gifts given by family

What are the appropriate procedures?

The couple kneels with the groom on the left of the bride.

The groom faces the father of the bride and the bride faces her mother.

The groom is first to serve tea. He serves the bride's father first and then her mother, saying, "Father, please drink the tea." "Mother, please drink the tea".

The bride takes her turn to serve tea, again to her father first and then her mother. The same words are spoken

Note: serving & receiving tea or gifts must be done with both hands

Helpful pointers on the order of service in presenting the tea:

1. Parents: Serve the bride's side first as above. Once all of her side has been completed the groom proceeds with his family
2. Grandparents
3. Grand-uncles and grand-aunties
4. Uncles and Aunties
5. Elder brothers and sisters
6. Elder cousins

Note: The father's relatives are served before the mother's relatives

Helpful point: A tea ceremony will be smoothest if there are three people to handle the duties. One person to hold tea and gifts on the plate or in the basket while the second person hands the tea to the participant. The third person to ensures there is always enough warm tea to refill the small tea pot.

Hindu Wedding Ceremonies

Below I am sharing a ceremony that was created for a multi-faith wedding where the groom was Indian, and bride was Roman Catholic. They wanted to capture some of his traditions and make it as special as possible. They chose the Fire ceremony and entrusted his brother-in-law and her brother-in-law to prepare and carry the fire to the sacred space. This allowed both sides of the family to be honored and involved.

GATH BANDHAN & PHERE

Officiant:

We are now going to move to a few very special Hindu traditions. With this flame, we invite the fire Gods to witness the marriage. Fire, a purifying agent, is also a source of energy. Only fire can separate this bond of unity between Bride and Groom. The couple will walk around the sacred fire seven times, making it a witness of their union as Husband and Wife.

While circling the fire, _____ and _____ are joined together by tying a corner of their outer garments, symbolizing the bond of marriage.

In the **first** round, _____ and _____ pray to the gods that they will provide them with pure and plentiful food. They ask for the strength to live life together and to always respect each other. They will support one another through good and bad, will nourish each other, and will always be mindful of each other's needs.

In the **second round,** _____ and _____ pray to the gods that they will give them the ability to understand each other. They promise that from today onwards, they are one entity rather than two separate people. They will now be the same, spiritually, mentally and physically, and will grow as a single force. They will build a home, ensuring that it is always full of happiness and laughter.

In the **third round,** they request the gods give them the strength to love each other selflessly and to understand the true meaning of marriage. Both _____ and _____ promise that they will never be selfish. They will selflessly love each other and their family. This will deepen their love and give them the strength to live life. They will always be together.

_____ will now lead _____ for the final four rounds. (It is customary that Bride now leads)

The **fourth round** has a very significant role in the social structure of the Indian culture. The Indian culture believes that marriage is not about two people, but about two families. In this round, they pray to the gods to give them the ability to accept each other's families. _____ and _____ promise each other that they will take responsibility of the elders in the family. They will take care of each other's parents and respect them. This will ensure that their home is blessed.

In the **fifth round,** _____ and _____ ask the gods to bless them with healthy children. They promise each other to take good care of their children and to teach them good values. They will consider the children as gifts from the gods, will nurture them well, and will ensure they are provided with a happy family home.

In the **sixth round,** the bride and groom pray to the gods for a healthy, disease-free life so that they can live prosperously. They promise to take care of one another, and to always be by each other's side till death does them part.

The **seventh and final round around the holy fire is the most** significant. The couple asks the gods to give them maturity and patience to understand each other. They promise to always love unconditionally and to mutually trust one another. These are the basic pillars of a strong and happy marriage.

Another prayer may be used

With the first step, we will provide for and support each other.
With the second step, we will develop mental, physical, and spiritual strength.
With the third step, we will share the worldly possessions.
With the fourth step, we will acquire knowledge, happiness, and peace.
With the fifth step, we will raise strong and virtuous children.
With the sixth step, we will enjoy the fruits of all seasons.
With the seventh step, we will always remain friends and cherish each other

Filipino Wedding Ceremonies

The first time I performed a Filipino wedding, I was overcome with how many sponsors the couple had. It only made sense later why there were so many parts to their ceremony as they wanted everyone involved. Even the children, who walk down the aisle with the family Bible.

In my travels to the Philippines, I went to purchase some extra cords, veils and coins for future weddings. I was dismayed to discover the shops had either just sold their last ones or the veils were yellow due to aging. I decided I would prefer the bride to purchase three meters of new lace fabric from a craft shop in Toronto than resort to that. I did have some luck at the last shop in Manilla, where I found a very beautiful cord. I have that in my office for use in those just-in-case moments.

Below is the ceremony with the use of all four practises:

- Candle
- Veil
- Cord
- Coins

Officiant:
We are now going to have the symbols of marriage and tradition to be presented and honoured

Candle Lighting Ceremony

The mothers come up

Would the mothers come forward now, light the tapers and present them to _____ and _____, as a symbol of your love and support.

_____ and _____ The taper candles represent your lives until this day, individual and unique. Would you, together with a single flame from the two candles, light your Wedding Candle.

Let this single flame be a symbol of illumination to light the way for you through your married life together.

Let the light remind you to cherish each living moment together, savour every breath and grow with each experience.

Veil Ceremony

Officiant:
Speaks to the sponsors asking them to come forward to help the Officiant.

_____ and _____, I ask _____ and _____ to join us.

They will have the honour of laying a veil over you both to clothe you together.

Let this be a symbol of the faithful love you have for each other.

Through the passing of the years, let the veil remind you that you belong to each other and to no one else.

Instructions: (Sponsor A) will clip the veil on the groom's right shoulder, while Sponsor B will drape the veil over bride's head and clip it on the bride's left shoulder

Cord Ceremony

Officiant:
_____ and _____ I call _____ and _____ to come up and help with the cord ceremony

_____ and _____ will place a cord over you. This cord symbolizes an infinite bond of love you share that keeps your relationship strong in the face of adversity, as well as symbolizing that you are no longer two, but one in marriage.

May this cord remind you to face your life together courageously and to be mutually supportive of each other's duties and responsibilities as a couple, and, may your love grow stronger & bind you closer together through the years.

Instructions: _____ will place the cord over _____'s head and rest it on his shoulders, while_____ will place the cord over _____'s head and rest it on her shoulders.

Coin Ceremony

Officiant:

_____ and _____, I ask the father of the bride to come up and present the coins to the **Officiant.**

This tradition stems from the understanding of husband as "bread winner "and wife as "home maker", so the coins were given and received not in a spirit of mutuality but in a give and take relationship.

Nowadays the coins are a reminder of good stewardship for all couples; that they will mutually support each other, their children & the community around them. May God bless these coins that symbolize mutual support and responsibility.

Officiant: will place the box in father's hands. Then the father will place the box into his son's hands. Then the son will give the box to the brides and then places his hands on top.

Officiant:

Turning to the groom

_____ repeat after me addressing the bride ... I give you this *arrhae* (coin) as a pledge of my dedication to your welfare.

Officiant:

Turning to the bride

_____ repeat after me addressing the groom… I accept them and in the same way pledge my dedication to you, the care of our home, and the welfare of our children.

Removal of Veil & Cord

I kindly ask the sponsors, _____ and _____ to remove the cord and veil.

Then they return to their seats.

Thank you.

Jewish Wedding Traditions

The Breaking of the glass

May be performed either after the exchange of rings or at the end of the wedding ceremony.

In honouring of tradition, we ask the Groom to break the glass (which has been covered with a cloth) with his right foot, as a symbol that joy must always be tempered.

Psalms 2:11, "Serve the Lord with fear, and rejoice with trembling."

Groom crushes the prepared glass or light bulb.

All shout "Mazel Tov!"

A Blessing of the wine and sharing your first drink together

The symbolism in Jewish faith is so beautiful that from a cluster of grapes one is able to make wine. Just as individuals, we unite in marriage and make one.

Wine is poured into a symbolic glass and the couple shares their first drink.

Bride goes first.

The Marriage Ring

The ring is usually of a solid metal like gold and with no precious stones.

Placed on the "Index finger" by the Groom, to show all that the Bride as received the ring. It may later be transferred to the "ring finger". The Bride also places Groom's ring on the "Index finger."

The Quaich (Quack) Ceremony

The Quaich is a traditional drinking cup which is unique to Scotland, drinking from a Quaich was part of a long-established tradition of hospitality. If you shared a cup like this with somebody, you couldn't do harm or injury to the other person so you got the term "Loving Cup". King James VI gifted this to his bride Anne of Denmark and thereafter sharing a Quaich became part of Scottish ceremonies.

_____ and _____ would like to continue with this tradition today. As their first act together as a married couple, they are going to drink from this Quaich. In doing so they are symbolising their commitment to sharing everything in life and sealing the bond between them, whilst signifying the blending of their families.

Officiant:
The years of your life together are like a cup of scotch poured out for you to drink. This Loving Cup contains within it a scotch, that its sweetness becomes your symbolic of happiness, joy, hope, peace, love and delight.

This scotch also has some bitter properties that are symbolic of life's trials and tribulations. Together the sweet and the bitter represent "Love's Journey" and all of the experiences that are a natural part of it. As you share the scotch, from this Loving Cup, so will you share all things in your life.

Both fathers walk up – One will hold the scotch, the other one the Loving cup.

One father pours drink into the Loving Cup and the other one holds it up.

Officiant:
This cup of scotch is symbolic of the cup of life. As you all share the scotch from the Loving cup, you undertake to share all that the future may bring.

All the sweetness life may hold for each you will be sweeter because you drink together. Whatever challenges it may contain will be less difficult because you share them. Drink now from this cup and acknowledge to one another that your lives have now become one.

The father who is holding the cup will pass it to _____ and _____.

Officiant:
Now drink to the love you've shared in the past.

_____ and _____ sip from the Loving Cup.

Officiant:
Drink to your love in the present, on this your wedding day.

_____ and _____ sip from the Loving Cup.

Officiant:
And drink to your love in the future and forever more!

_____ and _____ sip from the Loving Cup and hand it back to one of the fathers.

Officiant:
As you have shared the scotch from the Loving Cup, so may you share your lives.

May you explore life's mysteries together and find life's joys heightened, its bitterness sweetened, and all of life enriched by the love of family and friends.

We will now have the fathers, as the heads of their clans, share a drink as well from the Loving Cup.

The Lasso Prayer and Blessing

Both mothers will come up. One mother will go to the table and pick up the lasso.

Both mothers stand by their children and together place the lasso over their heads and rest it on the couple's shoulders. They then step back a bit and couple will bend their heads during the blessing.

Officiant:
Bless the marriage of _____ and _____, O God, as they begin their journey down the road of life together. We know not what lies ahead for the road has many turns and bends.

We are grateful to you for helping them to make the best of whatever comes their way.

We are thankful that they can continue to enjoy each other as they did when they first met and for helping them realize that nothing nor no one is perfect and to look for the good in all things and all people including themselves.

Thank you for helping them to respect each other's likes and dislikes, opinions and beliefs, hopes and dreams and fears even though they may not always understand them.

Thank you for helping them to learn from each other and to help each other grow mentally, emotionally, and spiritually.

Thank you for helping them to realize that no matter what happens to them they will hold on to each other and know that things have a way of working out for the good.

Thank you for helping them to create for their children a peaceful, stable home of love as a foundation on which they can build their lives.

But most of all, dear God, thank you for helping them to keep lit the flame of love that they now share so that by their loving example they may pass on the light to their children and to their children's children forever and ever.

And so it is.

The mothers remove the lasso and give it to the bride as a memento of her becoming the mistress of the groom's heart and home. The bride will then pass the lasso to the officiant who will place it on the table.

Jumping the Broom

My research discovered that jumping the broom was performed in England, United States, South Africa and Ghana during the early 19th century as a marriage ceremony, for couples that were not allowed to wed legally. This ceremony became very popular again in the 1970's due to the novel and movie Roots.

Require:
- One broom that may be decorated with ribbons and stings

Officiant:
"The bride and groom have chosen to conclude this ceremony with the tradition of jumping the broom.

Today, we honour and celebrate the transition of two separate, thriving lives into one cohesive unit – bound by love, trust and passion. The leap they take together is also symbolic, by taking this leap they make the gesture of dedication to working together while sweeping away of the old and welcoming the new."

Officiant: Can family member or friend, please hand the broom to Groom.

Officiant: "Groom, give it a good sweep and hand the broom to Bride who will place it on the floor in front of the two of you".

Officiant:
"Now, sharing a life with another person requires many leaps of faith. Jumping the broom symbolizes a leap of faith that Bride and Groom have chosen, they're jumping into a new life with the solemn promise to protect and support each other. By jumping, they work together through the tough times ahead – as well as

the easy times. They also leave behind the past and jump into the future together secure in their love."

The jump is also a call of support for the marriage from the entire community of family and friends.

Everyone, please count "1, 2, 3… jump!" together with me and shout with joy as they perform their first act of working together as husband and wife.

1, 2, 3…. JUMP!

Chapter Seven
REHEARSALS (OR NOT)

Walkthroughs are the best thing to calm the nerves. Nerves are a common concern with most couples as they wonder how the ceremony will unfold. My job that day will be to ensure that you both are present and ready to enjoy the moment fully. Many people are nervous about standing in front of so many others. I remind you that you have invited these people and that they are attending the ceremony because they are your family and friends, and they are there to support your union. This is why I so enjoy the walk-through package before the big day for small bridal parties and rehearsals for six or more bridal members.

What is a walk through?

We will meet and walk through the steps of the entire wedding ceremony.

In a ceremony we have several parts and they all have a proper name.

1. The Processional
2. Opening Remarks

3. Readings (Note: the more readings the longer the ceremony)
4. Exchange of Vows
5. Exchange of Rings or watches, as a sign of their commitment
6. The signing of the marriage register
7. The Declaration of Marriage
8. The Kiss
9. The Recessional

Processional

Once all the guests have been seated and the couple is ready, the procession starts.

Have you selected the music to set the mood of your wedding?

Actual musicians, a DJ, or a friend holding a cell phone can help provide the music to accompany the order of the bridal party's entrance. How you want to walk down the aisle is up to you.

Does the groom go first? With or without his both parents, just his mother or by himself?

How will the bridal party present themselves? Will the groomsmen stand at the front with the groom in waiting or escort the bridesmaids?

Maybe even a "pop up style ", everyone gathers around the couple.

We experience the flow together.

The bride holds her bouquet in different positions in order to decide which way works the best. How will she be presented: by her father, brother, uncle, mother, an alternate or solo. How would you like to be introduced to your partner? What are you going to do with your bouquet? (Personal preference, you are marrying your partner not your bouquet. I prefer my couples hold each other's hands and not the flowers). Yes, these are all minor issues but when you compound them within a short span of time, they can be overwhelming.

Opening Remarks

Once the couple has reached the sacred space, how do they stand? What do they look at after the opening remarks are made? I provide guidance and we move around to get the feel of the ceremony. At this point in the actual ceremony, we welcome everyone and provide a brief intro about the couple.

I have witnessed the way too many couples feel uncomfortable and I really try my best to have them welcome the new experience with fun and ease. As I prefer not to read the script during the walk through or rehearsal, the "Blah Blah Blah", moments are introduced and never forgotten.

Readings

Guidance is provided on how to stand and receive the messages from the readings, especially if you have chosen a loved one to read. Last summer, a couple chose three readings to be read by the elder women of the family. This was so powerful! It started with the aunts and ended with the grandmother, *nonna*, in her mother language, Italian. All the ladies chose to stand next to the couple. The love and support was felt throughout the venue and there wasn't a dry eye! As for me, I prefer to stand at the side so that all eyes are on the two of you. The more readings you have chosen, the longer the ceremony.

Vows Exchange

This is the fun part! If the couple has decided to read their own vows, this is the spot where I hand them out as each one finishes their part. The cards are then placed on the signing table as keepsakes. To be honest, there have been weddings where I have been so caught up with the couple's energy, I forget to hand them over and have to mail the cards the following week.

Exchange of Rings

Since I have arrived early, I now know who has the rings and will make eye contact with them when the moment arrives. I will ask them to kindly place the rings in the palm of my hands and then perform a blessing on them. Once completed, I ask the couple to pick up their partner's ring. No matter how many times I have done this, there is always a person who wants to pick up their own.

After, I will instruct them on how to properly place the ring on their partner's finger as they proclaim their intentions. The hardest part for me is to make sure the couple does not kiss. We are not done yet! Thank goodness I have fast reflects and have stopped many!!!

Signing the Marriage Register

Everyone can take a breath now as we are almost done. The couple and their witnesses walk over to the signing table where the marriage licence and marriage registry are awaiting to be completed. This is a great moment to make sure there is some music in the background to entertain your guests for the next few minutes. My preference here is to have only one chair for one person to be seated. The photos look so good with the other partner beside them. Once they have signed the documents, we ask the witnesses to take their spots and complete the paperwork. The documents are verified and signed off by the officiant. Everyone returns to their proper spots for the final stage.

The Declaration of Marriage

This is a legal requirement that only an officiant has the power to declare. Just like in the movies, "It is with the power of the province, that I hereby declare you husband and wife."

The Kiss

The moment you have all been waiting for has finally arrived! Once declared, the kiss seals the deal.

And yes, there are fun ways to make this moment yours. That is what a walkthrough is all about! There are no pecking kisses at my ceremonies!!!

The Recessional

The party starts! Choose a great song to walk down that aisle together, as a newly married couple.

The new couple walks the whole length of the aisle by themselves. They are followed by the bridal party, the parents, and then the guests. If there are any special instructions as to where you would like family to go for photos, or that everyone can go to the bar, let the officiant know beforehand so that the instructions may be introduced at the start and again at the end, as guests like to have guidance.

There have been many times after we have completed the walk through that either the groom, or bride, or both say to me that they had no idea what to expect but now feel more at ease about their ceremony.

What is the difference between a walk through and a rehearsal?

If you have a large bridal party and need help to train the group, or know that too many chefs spoil the pot, I am delighted to meet everyone before the wedding at your venue or where-ever we agree. There have been occasions where the space and the size of the bridal party had not been considered. When everyone was present, changes were easily addressed and revised before the big day.

As I love children, this gives me the opportunity to introduce myself to your ring boys and flower girls. Kids get very nervous sometimes with so many strangers watching them. By them seeing and now knowing who I am, they can focus on looking at the front with some comfort as well the day of the wedding.

Rehearsals are a separate fee of $150.00 to $180.00 depending on the location but worth it if you want everyone on the same page. I make it fun and I do not leave until we all agree with how the ceremony will unfold and that everyone understands their roles during the wedding ceremony. Plus, there is nothing more rewarding than seeing the couple and their friends laughing and making memories. The fun part for me is during the wedding, as we have made a connection the day before, we are all comfortable and smiles when the ceremony is in play.

Note: I have performed ceremonies where no walk though or rehearsals have been performed due to timing or costs and I still did my best for the couple to feel comfortable and enjoy the moment.

Chapter Eight
THE BIG DAY

What to expect from a professional wedding Officiant.

The big day has arrived! All the planning has paid off and everyone is here to make it happen. My suggestion to all my couples is please have a good breakfast which includes protein (shakes are perfect) that day as you will be so busy and will not have time to eat later. As well, please drink water so that you don't get dehydrated. I have attended a few where the couples were so tired and moody because of these reasons that they couldn't enjoy their day fully. You can always assign a bridesmaid and best man to the task of reminding everyone as well.

My role as a wedding officiant is to arrive 30 to 45 minutes before the ceremony. I will find you both and make sure that everything is ready to go. You will hand me the marriage licence or leave it on the signing table.

I will:

- introduce myself to the event planner, if you have one;
- find the photographer and make sure we are on the same page;

- check that the signing table is set up with a chair and in a good location; as well get a glass of water ready for the couple just in case
- locate the best man and the rings; and
- find the DJ and make sure the microphone is working.

In one ceremony, we had tested the microphone, and all was good to go. However, during the ceremony we had to change the microphone twice and I ended up just speaking as loud as I could. Life happens and we all laughed.

In my previous job, I was an auditor for a bank and personal security was my speciality. Crazy but true. I have an eye for possible threats and help reduce or eliminate any dangers.

Let me share some more stories.

August 2018. It was a very wet summer and rain appeared every weekend. Upon my arrival to this particular wedding, the couple had decided to have the wedding ceremony under a canopy along the side of the restaurant. This was a lovely plan however the floor and the side chairs were all wet. The event planners had the staff wipe the area where they felt it was required. My requirements were a bit different—safety first. The spot where the bride and groom would be standing was still wet and the side chairs where covered with rain drops. Noticing this, I asked the staff for help and they quickly dried the areas. The bride and groom stayed comfortable and no damage was done to her shoes or dress. Plus, all of the chairs were used and everyone was able to enjoy the ceremony in comfort.

It was a beautiful sunny Saturday afternoon of May 2019 and everything was in play for an indoor ceremony. The event planner had been hired and placed several tall glass containers holding lit candles along the aisle and at the front where the wedding was to take place. It looked spectacular! Then the family was allowed in and within five minutes, one of the containers was hit accidently and broke into pieces. I quickly called the staff to clean up and they did the best they could. Once they were done, I walked over and found several pieces of broken glass where the bridal party was going to walk.. I took a cloth and cleaned it myself as the wedding was about to start. We all understand what could have happened to the women as they all had open toes shoes!

Back in 2019, I was hired by two very busy medical personal. They found each other later in life as their passion for helping others was their main purpose, that is until love arrived! The wedding and rehearsal where held at the new hotel in Toronto, the XHotel by the Lake Ontario. Just gorgeous but parking a challenge. On arrival. I was introduced to the event planner, family and friends that were there. Upon entering the vast glass enclosed venue, I was overtaken by the simplicity and elegance of the room. Old world below and new above. I was walking on glass floors that overlooked the historical finds below. Beautiful.

Doing what I always do, I started to inspect the surroundings for any safety concerns, as family and friends were talking. My gaze travelled from the glass floor to up to the glass ceilings and then I saw it, one very large glass panel, located on the top right side of the ceiling, was shattered and had no protection below it! Not safe. My next steps were to inform the couple, who were so surprised and relieved that I detected it before the wedding. The groom even said to the event planner "This is why we hired Mary!" I felt appreciated. The next day, as people were seating in the venue, I ensured that no one sat under that panel, as neither the event planner nor the hotel had provided any precautions. The thought of anyone under that space did not sit well with me. The wedding ceremony went undisturbed and the couple were all smiles the whole time.

Once the ceremony is completed and all documents have been signed. I am required by law to mail the marriage licence to government office. My personal preference is to scan the marriage licence and email this to the couple for their own personal file. It is the couples' responsibility to request the marriage certificate, which may be obtain by going to Service Ontario for details. Note that depending on the season may take up to twelve (12) weeks to obtain.

Sample Marriage Certificate:

CERTIFICATE OF MARRIAGE

ON THIS DAY
IN THE CITY OF
PROVINCE OR STATE OF

And

TOOK EACH OTHER BY THE HAND AND JOINED THEIR LIVES TOGETHER BEFORE THE UNIVERSE, FAMILY AND FRIENDS AND DECLARED THEMSELVES TO BE UNITED IN MARRIAGE TO EACH OTHER AND VOWED TO LOVE, RESPECT, HONOUR AND SUPPORT EACH OTHER.
WITH TRUTH AND INTEGRITY, THEY CELEBRATE THEIR PLEDGE
BY SIGNING BELOW

| SIGNS | BRIDE | SIGNS | GROOM |

| WITNESS SIGNS | WITNESS SIGNS |

Wedding Officiant signs   *Date*

Music helps to set the tone of your ceremony

Part of planning the ceremony also includes finding the right music:

    a. Processional Songs

    b. Song as the Bride walks down the Aisle

    c. Song when the signing of legal documents takes place

    d. Recessional song

Here are 20 songs to start with if you have no idea of what to choose.

"Peace" by O.A.R.
"I choose You" by Sara Bareilles
"Mary Me" by Train
"You are the reason" by Calum Scott/ Leona Lewis
"All my Life" by K-Ci and JoJo
"On This Day" by David Pomeranz
"When I Dream at Night" by Marc Anthony
"Beautiful In White" by Matt Johnson, Acoustic Hits, Vol.3
"It's You" by Michelle Branch, Hotel Paper
"As Love is My Witness" by Westlife, Where We Are
"I Do" by Colbie Caillat
"This Is How We Do It" by Montell Jordan
"Raise Your Glass" by P!nk
"Because You Love Me" by Celine Dion
"I knew I Love You" by Savage Garden
"Perfect" by Ed Sheeran
"All You Need is Love" by The Beatles
"Somewhere Over the Rainbow" by Israel
"Can't Help Falling in Love " by Haley Reinhart
"Ave Maria" by Schubert

The "Whoops" moments!

In closing, sometimes with all the best planning the whoops moments happen. Some of them are controllable, other are not. Here are some of my most common controllable ones. Enjoy!

1. Lost Wedding Rings

Crazy but true, this has happened a few times with me. Remember when I mentioned that one of my 'to do' things when I arrive early to the wedding ceremony is to check to see who has the rings? Well this is why. My adorable couple back in 2018, had a full house of family members from Ireland who came for the wedding. Their wedding was taking place over on one of the Islands off of Toronto. They had a lot of preparing to do and tons of bags filled with decorations for the banquet hall. Needless to say, they were overwhelmed! When I arrived, I proceeded to do my job and discover that they can't find them! We had a "what!" moment! Rather than using his mom's ring which was kindly offered, the bride quickly decided to turn her engagement ring around and *voila* no one knew the difference when the ceremony was done!

The funny thing, two weeks after family returned home to Ireland, my adorable couple found the rings in the bottom of one of the Dollarama plastic bags still in their boxes!! They called me to let me know and I invited them over to my home to perform a hand blessing with the rings on. A very magical moment for us all!

2. Best Man does not show up

A good idea is to make sure everyone in the bridal party travels together or at least arrives at the venue at the same time. In one case, the wedding was taking place at noon in The Distillery District, in Toronto. Everyone was there but the best man who was the bride's brother. We waited and waited. As I do not book my weddings too close together for just these reasons, we were able to wait 20 minutes. After that the bride decided to go ahead without him. She chose another family member to witness and sign the documents. He showed up after the wedding ceremony was completed. Never knowing traffic situations, please make sure everyone has a head start and directions.

3. Left Marriage Licence at home

This has happened a few times!! My best suggestion is to have a wedding day binder or bag for that day. As you gather things for that your wedding day, place that item in there and you will have one place to look for all your important items. These can be things like the envelopes to pay the vendors, gifts for your bridal party, and the marriage licence.

When the couple realized that the marriage licence was left at home, the groom drove back to get it. They were lucky as I did not have another wedding after them that Thanksgiving Weekend, just my family waiting for me to serve the turkey dinner.

Another couple had to wait to get the forms signed later that day as I did have another wedding and quickly met up with them to complete with their witnesses.

4. Last but real, divorced parents who don't follow instructions

Being a divorced parent, I have heard and seen many situations where sometimes as adults we have to remember that this is not our day but our children's. I am hired by the couple getting married and give my help, and provide support, to them 100 per cent.

We work together to make their day the way they want and keeping everyone in mind. Especially those parents that do not talk to each other after their divorce.

In one wedding ceremony, the bride's mother refused to sit where the bride wanted her to sit during the ceremony. This really made matters very uncomfortable for the bride. I did try a few times very politely asking the mother to move, but she refused. The brides' dad wins the code of honour that day as he sat at the end of the row with a smile watching his daughter get married.

In another wedding ceremony, the first row was completely empty during the wedding ceremony as both bride and groom parents were divorced and remarried. During the walkthrough the week before, the bride had mentioned that she wanted both her dads to walk her down the aisle, which I thought as so beautiful and honouring of them both. They were working with an event planner, so I didn't ask any further questions. Something, I will know to keep in mind always!

Sometimes, the best laid plans have to be tossed out the window when a completely uncontrollable event occurs.

COVID-19 and Pandemic Weddings

In the start of the 2020 wedding planning, I was fully booked for the summer and into the fall. I had a few weddings in March and I was ready to celebrate. However, the world had different plans. In a matter of days Toronto was under lock down and the Covid-19 virus was hitting many countries harder than others. In Ontario, the government decreed that we were not allowed to perform any weddings. Toronto City Hall stopped issuing marriage licence, unless it was an emergency situation. The last wedding ceremony I performed was on April 4 2020, with only five people present, all wearing face masks.

I started to receive calls daily from my couples wondering what they should do about their weddings and if I was going to charge them extra for changing the day. My heart was not comfortable with charging extra for something my couples couldn't control. Something that I so enjoy and love to do was taken away from me and my wonderful couples without choice. We had to all follow the rules for safety of ourselves and others.

The next few weeks were filled with calls from my summer and fall weddings, postponing and rescheduling. There were weeks when I could not even look at my files as I had no idea what was going on.

Everyone was affected. Businesses not designated as essential services were closed. Many other wedding vendors had been greatly impacted and we all just starting to support each other. The one thing I learned during this crazy time was that the florist needed to be informed ASAP for they pay for the flowers ahead of time.

Once the numbers of COVID cases were reduced or the media proclaimed something about a curve being flattened or eliminated, everyone was longing for a form of normalcy, we were granted permission to perform weddings with a maximum of five people. It was only on June 12th, 2020 we were permitted to have ten people present (this includes the officiant, the couple, two witnesses and now a few chosen people, maybe a parent or two). The funny thing was that we could now perform the ceremony outside with fifty guests with social distancing, but only ten were allowed to stay for the reception. Who comes up with these numbers? I guess they hadn't attended a wedding ceremony in a while.

One of my postponed weddings for September 2020 couldn't wait any longer and they found a place outside of Toronto to get the marriage licence. We agreed to host a simple ceremony where the legal paperwork would be completed, and we would have the full ceremony with the wedding bands on a later date. As the stress and moving things around was a lot for us all, I chose not to charge my clients for this extra time and hope to celebrate with them again at their postponed date. On Saturday June 5, 2020 we performed a very intimate wedding ceremony with family (who didn't know they were getting married that afternoon) in their backyard. All were wearing shorts and casual attire. We had hand sanitizer, separate pens and masks, if needed. I left an hour later seeing everyone delighted to just be together and celebrating something wonderful. The couple will still be hosting their larger celebrations in October 2021.

The number of people allowed to be at the wedding ceremony was increased to 10 on June 12, 2020 which allowed me to perform another backyard wedding on Monday June 15, 2020. The weather once again was picture perfect and the couple were all smiles. The sisters of the couple had some fun shopping at Dollarama and created a very special space for the celebrations to take place.

Learning to change with the times has allowed me to create a pre wedding ceremony where I am using a local organic hand sanitizer to perform a hand blessing to all those in attendance. This has become quite popular and makes everyone feel safe. It has also provided me the opportunity to get to know each guest more than ever. At one wedding in July 2020, as I was blessing the guests' hands, I noticed that all the men had strong working hands with callouses. I asked why and they informed me that they were farmers. WOW! So wonderful to be surrounded by the people who put food on my table every day! I just had to use this new information in the ceremony. The opportunity presented itself. It was during the hand blessing that I made it a point to acknowledging the strength and the support of their hard-working family members that will always be there for the couple.

The one thing I have learned during these changing times, is that couples have become so accommodating and caring. Their focus has been on living in the moment. Whether it is having intimate backyard elopements, drive by hellos to friends, there are no more arguments that they can't get their way. I have asked all my couples to please be flexible with their ceremony times as so many weddings have been rescheduled. A great amount of gratitude for being able to either postpone or host an intimate venue at home has been so well received by all. Love has truly won this round of new change.

CONCLUSION

For the next few months before the wedding, start to notice words from music, movies, and books you read to help pull ideas for your wedding, be it for the vows to evening speeches. Enjoy the coming days with ease and excitement. You have been dreaming of this day your whole life. Make it unfold with love and joy. Things may go "wrong" and may not be exactly the way you wanted at the end or even better. Keep asking the Universe for help and slow down to listen. It doesn't matter if you are spending $500 on a wedding or $250,000. If there is no love, joy, laughter and peace in the chaos, was it worth it? Remember to make time for each other during these prep times to have fun as well. If you are feeling overwhelmed, communicate with each other, as your partner maybe feeling the same way.

As a wedding officiant, I am here to listen and provide the best service possible. I take pride in my work and it is my honour to celebrate and help make your day yours!

Big hugs,
Rev. Mary

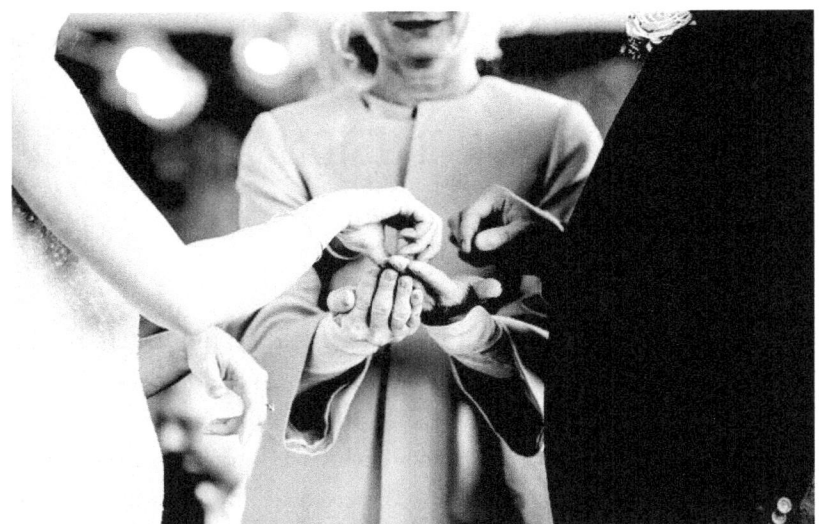

APPENDIX I

The Next Steps

If you would like to work with me, these are the Next Steps:

1. email me back with both of your full names, home addresses and cell numbers best to call on day of wedding
2. Date of wedding and time of ceremony
3. Full address of location/venue
4. The package you would like
5. A receipt will be issued once a 50 % retainer of that package has been e-transferred and processed to my business email mary@reverendmary.ca
6. Password for e-transfers may or may not be required
7. Once you have the marriage licence, kindly send me a scan of it, along with the full names and addresses of your 2 witnesses
8. May I have permission to share your wedding photo on my Instagram account: yes or no

9. The final payment: kindly e-transfer the morning of the wedding, the day before, or place cash in the marriage licence folder. Much appreciated.

Happy planning,
Mary
Reverend Mary Montanari
Registered Wedding Officiant for the Province of Ontario
Minister of CIMM

APPENDIX II
SERVICES & FEES

My fee for a regular Toronto wedding includes: a call or video (Zoom, Skype, Google Hangouts, WhatsApp) to learn about you as a couple and prepare the beginning of your customized ceremony. We build in all the legal and personal elements into the ceremony with unlimited video chats, emailing and calls. I perform the ceremony, complete all the legal paperwork, and send it to be processed. If the venue does charge for parking, please make sure to have this amount included in my payment that day as well or pay them directly.

Walk Through: When the ceremony is 90% complete, we arrange to meet in person (usually before the wedding, at my office) or on video chat to review the ceremony content, but also rehearse all the elements leading up and ending of the ceremony. At this meeting, you will bring the marriage licence you've picked up from city hall, and your 2 witnesses' addresses, so I can complete most of the paperwork, before the ceremony (who wants to watch me fill out papers during the wedding, when we are almost done?)

What is include in a walk through meeting - The walk through is not a rehearsal with extended family, or wedding party but just the three of us. It gives you the peace of mind to relax at your own wedding and to be able to conduct a rehearsal without me. You do not leave me till I hear and see your smiles. The average time is about 45mins. If after doing a walk through you wish to also have me attend a rehearsal to help with informing the members of the wedding party there is an extra charge and we make sure I do not leave till everyone is on the same page with smiles.

OTHER SERVICES

- # 1 Small Weddings under 10 people total in Toronto or city hall weddings
- # 2 Weddings in the GTA (Venue postal code must start with the letter 'M').
- # 3 Weddings in the GTA that include a walk through at my office or Zoom session
- # 4 Weddings on the Toronto Islands or Boats and couples must arrange transportation to and from the Island/Boat
- # 5 Weddings outside of Toronto and GTA can be negotiated based on distance
- # 6 Elopements / Paperwork (Basic legal requirements only)
  - simple service, travel to your place in the "M" postal code, with less than 5 guest
  - can hire 2 witnesses for a fee each if required
- # 7 Friends Officiating, costs vary

Note for a Very special Wedding Packages:

Package A: Signature (travel extra if not in the "M" postal code)

- Includes everything of the main Package
- Full rehearsal with family, bridal party at chosen location.
- Spiritual energy healing of 30 mins per person (Bride & Groom) to help reduce stress and allow them to fully enjoy their special day grounded and in peace.
- Keep sake of the ceremony: this year it is custom candle infused with holistic essential oils that may be used in the ceremony.

Package B: Premium (travel extra if not in the "M" postal code)

- Includes everything of the main Package
- Full rehearsal with family, bridal party at chosen location.
- Spiritual energy healing for 1 hour per person (Bride & Groom) to help reduce stress and allow them to fully enjoy their special day grounded and in peace.
- Keep sake of the ceremony: this year it is custom candle infused with holistic essential oils that may be used in the ceremony.

Please make sure that whomever you get as an Officiant that you check the Canadian Government site to make sure they are licensed. This is best preformed on a computer and not with your cell phone as their site is not mobile friendly. This was an issue in Niagara and again recently in Peterborough Toronto Star.

YOUR WEDDING – I arrive 30 minutes before the ceremony and coordinate with your wedding planner, musicians, DJ, readers, and wedding party to ensure everyone is on the same page.

You are responsible to obtain the marriage licence from any city hall. Good idea to start process online. You need to get the licence and this is a helpful site. https://www.ontario.ca/page/getting-married

Note: During Covid couples are required to book an appointment to pick up their marriage licence at the city hall of their choice.

The licence has a 90 day expiry. I suggest to my couples to get it at least 1 month before the wedding date.

REGISTRATION – You get married and I take care of the rest including completing all legal documentation, registering your marriage licence, sending you a copy, and archiving your registry.

NEXT Steps:

If you wish to book my services, you will need to send me an email to include: both of your full names, home addresses, phone numbers, the date, time and location of the wedding. Tell me which package price you prefer, along with a retainer of 50% (via e-transfer) that will hold my services with my licensing agency. A Freshbook receipt will be issued once I have received all information and the date is then reserved.

Happy Planning,

Mary
Rev. Mary Montanari
Minister of CIMM
Registered with the Ontario Government

RESOURCES

Helpful Books to help define your relationships

Buscaglia Leo, *Loving Each Other, The Challenge of Human Relationships*, Thorofare, New Jersey: SLACK Incorporated, copyright 1984

Chapman Gary, *The 5 Love Languages, The Secret to Love That Lasts*, Oasis Audio

Hendrix, Harville and LaKelly, Helen, *Making Marriage Simple, 10 TRUTH for CHANGING the RELATIONSHIP YOU HAVE into the ONE YOU WANT*, New York, Harmony Books, copyright 2013

Hendrix, Harville and LaKelly, Helen, *Receiving Love, TRANSFORM YOUR RELATIONSHIP BY LETTING YOURSELF BE LOVED*, New York, Atrica Books, copyright 2004

Ruiz, Don Miguel, *THE FOUR AGREEMENTS*, San Rafael, CA, Amber-Allen Publishing Inc. copyright 1997

Wedding Planners

Pastiche/Weddings & Events. www.pasticheevents.ca

Trade Sensation Events & Co. www.tradesensation.com

International Wedding Planner www.envisionweddings.ca

Marble Weddings www.marbleweddings.com

Paulette Escoe-Grant www.parties365.com

Something Blue/Event Planner www.SomethingBlueEvents.ca

CHECKLISTS FOR WEDDING PREPARATION

These are the key ingredients of a memorable wedding. You can do them in the order that suits your preferences and requirements.

- Book the venue
- Secure Wedding Officiant
- Hire an event planner if desired
- Flowers
- Photographer
- Hair stylist
- Make-up artist
- Wedding rings
- Obtain the wedding licence
- Attire for the day: Dress, suit, groomsmen and bridesmaids
- Honeymoon
- Music: live performers and DJ
- Order the cake or chosen dessert
- Invitations and thank you cards
- Transportation

- Bonbonnieres or party favors
- Rehearsal and possible dinner after with bridal party
- There may be a few of your own personal goals

Look at some of your other books for ideas about what you want to say here.

The Bag for the day

There will be so much going on that day that most couples either go with the flow or lose it. So far, I have been blessed to be with couples that go with the flow! Below is a list of items that my years of being a mom and officiant have proven truly save the day.

Have a personal bag and the event bag. The personal bag will carry all your items that are readily available for you if you have to run to the change room. Make sure you assign this care to a person that can carry it during the day and that will be near you always.

- Extra underwear, sanitary supplies and stockings
- Perfume
- Baby powder
- Tide to Go™ stick
- Hair pins
- Safety pins
- Clear nail polish
- Nail file
- Shoes and slippers
- Needle and thread set
- Makeup

- Tissues
- Cotton pads
- Hand cream
- Lip bam
- Lipstick
- Lace Handkerchief for that Feminine touch
- Small wallet with cash and credit card
- Scissors
- Deodorant
- Snacks
- Water
- Towel

The Event Bag

Great to carry:

- The Agenda with contact phone numbers
- Marriage Licence
- Rings
- Envelopes for vendor payments
- Dinner speeches
- Phone charger

ABOUT THE AUTHOR

Rev. Mary Montanari is a spiritual teacher and writer working and living in Toronto, Ontario. This is her first book which will be followed by her memoir in 2021. She has an active podcast station created during the Covid-19 Pandemic to help her local and international clients deal with the changes via meditations. She always feels at home when she sees a bottle of chilled Veuve Clicquot. Loves traveling, trying new recipes, gardening, her dog Cloe, and playing 80's music really loudly in her home or car. She is the proud mother of four successful adults, who are just as passionate as she is when it comes to helping others and keeping the world a better place to live.

Instagram: mary.montanari
Website: www.reverendmary.ca
Podcast: Traveling within with Mary

NOTES

Made in the USA
Middletown, DE
28 October 2020